PRAISE FOR *HOLISTIC HOMESTEADING*

"If you want to live off the land and grow a regenerative homestead, this book is a great primer into essential steps: from siting your garden and understanding design principles to wild foraging and home preserves. Roxanne is full of good advice!"

—**Zach Loeks, director of the Ecosystem Solution Institute and author of *The Permaculture Market Garden* and *The Edible Ecosystem Solution***

"In *Holistic Homesteading*, Roxanne Ahern lays out the why and the how of living a more grounded and meaningful existence through the simple, beautiful, everyday acts of home production. It was once commonplace for our ancestors to mark the days and the seasons through the production happening in the home: the flush of the summer garden, the work of storage in autumn, the renewal and abundance of spring, the simple dance between human culture and animal husbandry and the delicate care of the plant world. *Holistic Homesteading* invites us back in to participate in this most essential and meaningful of human tasks: the work and joy of making a living from the land and reveling in its abundance."

—**Dr. Ashley Colby, environmental sociologist, director of Rizoma Field School, and author of *Subsistence Agriculture in the US: Reconnecting to Work, Nature and Community***

"*Holistic Homesteading* offers a wide array of information on finding land, starting a homestead, and enjoying the rhythms of a land-based lifestyle. Filled with practical tips and important things to consider along the way, it's a perfect book for inspiration at any point in your homesteading journey."

—**Tao Orion, Resilience Permaculture Design, LLC, author of *Beyond the War on Invasive Species: A Permaculture Approach to Ecosystem Restoration***

HOLISTIC HOMESTEADING

A Guide to a **Sustainable** and **Regenerative** Lifestyle

HOLISTIC HOMESTEADING

A Guide to a **Sustainable** and **Regenerative** Lifestyle

BY ROXANNE AHERN

yellow pear press
CORAL GABLES, FL

Cover Design & Art Direction: Morgane Leoni
Cover Photo: valya82/Adobe Stock
Layout & Design: Katia Mena
Images used under license of Adobe Stock

For permission requests, please contact the publisher at:
Mango Publishing Group
2850 S Douglas Road, 4th Floor
Coral Gables, FL 33134 USA
info@mango.bz

For special orders, quantity sales, course adoptions and corporate sales, please email the publisher at sales@mango.bz. For trade and wholesale sales, please contact Ingram Publisher Services at customer.service@ingramcontent.com or +1.800.509.4887.

Holistic Homesteading: A Guide to a Sustainable and Regenerative Lifestyle

Library of Congress Cataloging-in-Publication number: 2022939088
ISBN: (print) 978-1-64250-995-3, (ebook) 978-1-64250-996-0
BISAC category code GAR022000, GARDENING / Techniques

Printed in the United States of America

This book is for the microbes.

Their important work was unnoticed for most of human history, and we are currently only beginning to scratch the surface. Let them be a reminder to keep looking closer, and to never underestimate the power of things we do not yet understand.

TABLE OF CONTENTS

INTRODUCTION

What is holistic homesteading? What makes it different than regular homesteading? What do I mean by a sustainable and regenerative lifestyle? To me the word *homesteader* describes anyone who works toward self-sufficiency. The definition need not be limited to folks who grow every bite of food they eat themselves and only wear things they make while living in a home they fashioned with their own hands. Although, if this is you, you have my unyielding respect.

A homesteader is a person who makes an effort to learn skills that will enable them to be more self-sufficient. This can manifest differently for different people based on their interests and abilities. A homesteader might want to grow and/or preserve food, build things, practice animal husbandry, learn how to butcher or cure meat, sew or crochet, the list goes on.

In our modern world, I do not believe that it is necessary to live on acreage to be a homesteader. There are suburban and urban homesteaders who live in subdivisions and apartments who are more capable than I am at many homestead-type skills. Inversely, many who own land are still perfectly content being completely reliant on supply chains entirely out of their control. Being a homesteader is not exclusive to the amount of land one has; instead, it is a mindset.

Now that the meaning of the term "homesteader" has been established, let's explore what is meant by the words *holistic*, *sustainable*, and *regenerative*. Holistic describes a way of looking at situations in which we take entire systems into account, rather than trying to understand them based on their isolated parts. Sustainable practices could continue without compromising the ability of future generations to meet their needs. Regenerate means to regrow, generate anew, or be reformed or reborn. In the last several generations (and some would argue since the beginning of human agriculture, but that debate is beyond the scope of this book), our planet and our bodies have been in a state of *degeneration*. We have used methods that are reductionist and admittedly unsustainable. We have continuously tilled the earth for thousands of years, which has annihilated soil life and reduced the nutritional value of our food. More recently in human history we have taken to pouring pesticides, herbicides, and chemical fertilizers onto the soil.

These chemicals have made their way into our bodies and have taken their toll. Not to mention the pollutants and chemicals in our water, air, and personal care products. The use of packaging and the amount of fuel that goes into simply transporting products from one place to another creates more pollution.

My homesteading journey began with personal health. I felt unwell and had a litany of health issues until I went on a retreat for a week around the age of twenty. They provided the food, all high-quality and healthy, and I felt like an entirely new person afterward. I became keenly aware of how the food I ate directly impacted the way I felt. This experience changed the course of my life. I began pursuing a career in holistic nutrition, which eventually led me to soil health because I quickly learned it didn't matter how many "healthy foods" are piled on a person's plate; food grown on soil barren of vitamins and minerals is also barren of vitamins and minerals. Animal products derived from animals raised on feedlots or in confinement houses and fed genetically modified grain and pumped full of antibiotics and growth hormones cannot nourish us in the same way as animals that are allowed to forage, express the characteristics innate to their species, and have access to fresh air and sunshine.

The *holistic homesteader*, then, works not just toward self-sufficiency but also toward restoring the health of their body and the earth. They work to rebuild the humus in the soil and the microbiomes in their body. They avoid products and practices harmful to other people and the environment. When confronted with an unsavory side effect of a practice they were using, they resolve to find or create a new practice. They see the natural world as a partner meant to be respected, not an adversary to overcome.

Humans have done tremendous damage to the earth and their bodies over the last few generations. We have used chemicals in agriculture and in our homes, and have eaten foods sold to us under a pretext of safety, but now consequences of these actions have started mounting in the form of agricultural dead zones, animal extinctions, and increasing disease rates. It has become impossible to ignore the facts. Just as cigarettes were promised to be safe, right up until the moment big tobacco began paying out tremendous lawsuits (and even after), today's chemical and food companies will have to pay the piper at some point. For example, RoundUp is still sold at many stores, even after being ordered to pay out over $2 billion to cancer patients in a single year. Bayer still denies their product causes cancer and many people still use this product as I write this.

For the first time since 1915–1918, the human lifespan in the United States has decreased for three years in a row. The estimated causes of this are rising suicide rates, more drug overdoses, and increasing rates of liver disease. When researchers look at populations throughout the world that have the highest life spans, some of the factors these people have in common are a healthy diet of whole foods with little or no processed foods, active lifestyles, a sense of purpose that continues into old age, strong ties with family, friends, and community, and a healthy environment.

In the western world, we spend most of our time inside and away from people we love. We live on convenience food because busyness has somehow become equated with success. We rush children to activities to enrich them as if simply spending intentional time with them wouldn't. It is common not even to know our neighbors' names. Our nation has high obesity, cancer, diabetes, and mental illness rates. Our systems are clearly broken, that cannot possibly be denied, but there is still time to fix things if new systems are created and fresh paradigms are instilled.

As we reach a tipping point in terms of planetary and human health, it is important that we create and implement new systems and practices designed to create improvement, not maintain the status quo. Just like a sick person needs a higher level of care and nurturing, our bodies and the earth need nurturing now. When an ill person is not tended to, their condition often worsens, leading to hospitalization or death. Consider yourself a member of the triage for nature; under the loving care of our efforts, the world can and will heal. And so can we.

MANY LITTLE PEOPLE

A wonderful quote by Anwar Fazal says, "Little people doing little things in little places everywhere can change the world." I think it is important to remember, when looking at the enormous problems in the world feels overwhelming and insurmountable, in many cases, change initiates from the bottom up, not the top down. I hear people expressing their disappointment in large structures: corporations for being careless, governments for not legislating changes. And yes, that is frustrating and there should be accountability for corporations and governments. But we have allowed ourselves, as a people, to become dependent and beholden to entities that do not seem to have our best interests at heart. We have sacrificed our independence for convenience and the powers that be have poisoned our food, water, and air, while subjecting animals and humans to horrendous treatment so that people can buy inexpensive and convenient goods.

If people say, "No, I would rather grow my own food than buy food from a food system that pollutes. I would rather make my own clothes than buy something made by a child who works sixteen hours a day in a factory for pennies," then change can begin. If we stop buying their products, those problems will go away. It may take time, but if consumers become hypervigilant regarding the ethics and environmental standards of the companies they purchase their goods from, then the companies will have to bend to this or fade away because no one will buy their wares.

But just as we want them to be accountable for their behavior, we must also be accountable for ours. We can't expect governments and corporations to protect the environment and simultaneously support companies who pollute and abuse. That is a mixed message. We have to stand by our convictions and say no, even if it is inconvenient.

THE IMPORTANCE OF A RIGHT LIVELIHOOD

The future world we create should have a plan that includes access to the "right livelihood" for all. What is the right livelihood? It is a person's ability to support themselves—and a family if that is their goal—in such a way that will not impact other humans or the planet in a negative way. There are millions of jobs in our current economy in which people can earn a living, but unfortunately many of these jobs contribute to the destruction of our planet, put other humans in the position of working in sweatshops, or create other undesirable situations. It is damaging to the human psyche to do work in which we knowingly decrease the quality of life for others. The problem is that we all have bills to pay and many of us have children to support, so when it comes to protecting some faceless, nameless humans we have never met in a third-world country, or feeding our own families, many people make a choice to stop thinking about those faraway people (or places) and focus on their responsibilities to those they love in their own home.

Doesn't this seem like a terrible and absurd choice to make? Between personal success and exploiting distant people and lands? But this is a reality for most Americans. It isn't by choice that most people do not know where many of the products they buy come from, what kinds of chemicals are in them, or how they are produced. Most assume that if a product is available for sale, it must be safe and not produced under unfair conditions. Now people feel dependent on these cheap and convenient goods. To escape from this system, we need to stop participating in it by A) creating local economies in which activities are sustainable and mindful, and B) no longer working for or buying things from companies whose practices make a negative impact on the standard of life on our planet. This will push current corporations to make positive changes; if they don't and people refuse to work for them or buy their products, then they will disappear, opening the marketplace to businesses with ethical practices.

Local food systems and supply chains truly are the way to heal the planet and ourselves. When we actually know the people we buy our goods from, it creates more accountability. It also encourages relationships. It keeps our dollars in our communities. In 1910, 33 percent of the American population were farmers or farm laborers. A majority of households either were farms or had a member who worked on a farm. Today, less than 2 percent claim agriculture as their occupation. In just over one hundred years, we have become a nation that knows nothing about agriculture. Small farmers have virtually no voice, no power at the ballot box. Because of this, large corporations that sell seeds, chemicals, and processed junk food have taken over our food system. It's time to take it back.

The first couple of chapters of this book are focused on how to choose a homestead and start home enterprises. The later chapters focus on specific skills like gardening, food preservation, foraging, and working with sourdough culture. Start anywhere you like with what interests you the most and what is most applicable in your current situation.

I was not raised growing food, raising animals, canning, preserving, or learning to cook from scratch. I was brought up on processed foods and had zero idea of how to produce anything for myself. I think many of my peers are the same. Over the last handful of generations, homes shifted from being places of enterprise with gardens and workshops to being a place we sleep and consume entertainment and the labor of others. Whether you live on a thousand acres or in a studio apartment, this book is about bringing production back into the home and local community so that we can increase personal and local resilience. In doing so we can build a better system and live healthy, more integrated lives. I have found immense pleasure and satisfaction in learning how to be more self-reliant and I want to share everything I have learned so that other people can know that joy too. So let's go! I hope this book leaves you feeling empowered, optimistic, and knowledgeable about something new.

CHAPTER 1

PLANNING A REGENERATIVE FUTURE

It is important before setting out on any journey to create a plan. Yes, it is possible to just jump in the car and start driving without any destination in mind. While that road might lead to somewhere interesting and include fun adventures on the way, it could also lead to a dead end or somewhere that we never wanted to go.

Once you have decided that a more self-sufficient life is for you, it will be necessary to decide what can be done to earn a living. You may already have a small side hustle or hobby that you plan to grow into a business, or maybe you are still trying to figure that out.

Once you have decided on a plan, be ready for a transition or a waiting period. I would not recommend quitting a job with no money in the bank, hoping that a brand-new venture will be a smashing success immediately. Transition is key. Figuring out goals, creating a timeline, and implementing a strategy will be important elements of your transition. If it is possible to keep a job or save equivalent to one year's salary (two is even better) to help bridge the gap, I highly suggest it. Also, many farm/homestead income streams are seasonal, so it is possible to have more than one way to make an income (I strongly encourage it). Do not work yourself to the bone; build breaks for yourself when you plan your new life. Many farmers and homesteaders fall into the trap of never being able to leave the homestead. If travel and getting away are important, make sure to strategize this into the front end of your plan. If you're planning to raise livestock, for example, who will tend them when it is time for a vacation?

IDEAS FOR GENERATING INCOME
ON A HOMESTEAD OR FARM

- Grow enough veggies or fruit to sell. Also think value-added products, jellies, baked goods, tomato sauces
- Dried/dehydrated foods
- Bees for honey and wax to use for personal care products or candles
- Wool: If you keep sheep, you can sell wool. Spinning, dyeing, felting, and creating fiber art is another way of value-adding
- Cut flowers, bouquets, or subscriptions—you pick
- Preserved food
- Freshly baked bread
- Eggs, consider selling eating eggs, but also raising hatching eggs. This is especially profitable from rare or desirable breeds. Rainbow eggs, for example, are in high demand. This can make a dozen eggs go way up in value.
- Raising different kinds of fowl to sell: chickens, guinea hens, quail, geese, turkeys, peafowl, ducks, etc.
- Decorative gourds. Value add by making them into birdhouses or fairy houses.
- Restore secondhand items (furniture, clothing) to be repurposed or reused. I see this as a big one moving forward as there is just such an extreme excess of unnecessary goods, especially when new items are often not made as well as older items.
- Microgreens to sell to restaurants
- Farm parties or homestead/farm experiences for others, a little cabin that could be Airbnb to give people that homestead/farm feel
- Fruits and nuts from trees (this will take a while to establish as fruits and nut trees will take time to produce)
- Art made from natural and repurposed items
- Workshops/classes in an area of your expertise: Food preservation, cheese making, permaculture, mushroom log-making, tree grafting, etc.
- Pick-your-own orchard or berry patch, can be combined with a picnic experience
- Pumpkin patch

- Foraging tours
- Grow and sell mushrooms or mushroom logs
- Make clothing
- Tinctures
- Salves
- Personal care products: soap, shampoo bars, lotion
- Firewood

In addition to producing items, offering services can be an additional way to produce income:

- Edible landscape designer
- Nutrition consultant
- Meal planner
- Personal chef
- Permaculture designer/consultant
- Farm/homestead consulting and planning
- Interior decorating
- Organization specialist
- Tutor, instructor
- Doula
- Personal trainer
- Accountability coaching
- Gardener
- Arborist
- Seamstress
- Barber
- Repairman
- Mechanic
- Carpenter
- Electrician
- Plumber

Remember that many ways of earning an income from the land are seasonal, so pick a few areas of interest that can be focused on at different times throughout the year. The most difficult thing is to get your customer in the door, so to speak. Once you have developed a relationship with people who trust you and your products, they will probably be glad to check out some of your other offerings.

List of questions to help you define your goals and land needs:

- What do I want to produce?
- Do I live in a climate conducive to producing this?
- Do I need access to land to produce this?
- If not, what do I need access to?
- Is it possible to work or trade for what I need or do I need to buy it with physical money?
- Do I have a market or distribution network for the products I would like to produce?
- Create a marketing plan. Are there possible mentors that could guide me as I go through this process?
- Are there any local groups I could join that would be helpful to me from a knowledge or networking perspective?

PLANNING A BUSINESS

If you have never owned your own business, it can seem like an overwhelming task. You may not be sure where to begin. Some universities consult with small business owners at no charge. You can also pay a fee to an expert for consulting. There are also many excellent books and websites for you to research this topic yourself; I will add some in the resources section.

If you decide to start your own business, there are a series of steps:

1. **Come up with an idea.** What product or service would be valuable to your local community that you would also enjoy producing?

2. **Do market research** to make sure there is a demand for your business.

3. **Make sure your business can be conducted in an ethical and environmentally sound way.** Where will you source material? How is it produced? Is there an environmentally friendly way to dispose of the end result of your product and is the process environmentally friendly? If your business requires packaging, have you looked into the cost of compostable or zero-waste options? These questions can feel overwhelming and in our current economic model it may be difficult, but it is important to ask these questions and start looking more closely at the impact our businesses make and working to make that impact a positive one. This is an exciting opportunity for ingenuity and creativity.

4. **Make a business plan.** This should be as clear and detailed as possible, but also concise and ideally not more than a couple of pages. This plan will outline your product or service, the target demographic, an estimate of startup, an estimate of possible returns, and a marketing plan. Doing this helps crystalize your idea and it will also be necessary if you are looking for investors or loans to help fund your business or influencers and industry leaders to offer an endorsement. If you find yourself struggling with this step, free business planning templates can be found online.

5. **Come up with a name and form an entity.** This name should be unique to your business. You can search for trademarks on the internet. Legal service companies do this for a small fee; you can also hire an attorney to do this step. You may choose to run your business as a sole proprietorship or decide to form an LLC or some other type or entity. There are different pros and cons for each type of business structure. There is plenty of information for you to research this, or you can hire legal counsel. This is also a good time to seek out an accountant, unless you don't mind handling that portion of your business. An accountant may also have some input for you about which type of business structure makes the most sense.

6. **Create a marketing plan.** Much can be done to promote a business for free on social media. Writing articles for magazines or newspapers can also be a good way to promote your product or service. There are always television, radio, and billboard ads; however, that type of advertising can be expensive. You may also be able to promote your business at local establishments such as libraries, grocery stores, farmers markets, small business fairs, or by sponsoring a local event. Local small business networking meetings can be a good way to connect with other entrepreneurs whose customers might find value in your good or service. A small local newspaper can be a good place to advertise, and depending on what you are selling, you may even be able to get a writeup!

CHAPTER 2

CHOOSING YOUR HOMESTEAD: SITE AND SCALE

To figure out what kind of homestead you will create, try writing down your objectives and vision. Do you want to raise animals? Would a completely self-sufficient, off-grid situation be ideal? Or are you looking to decrease the environmental impact you make but enjoy living in close community with others in an urban or suburban area?

Becoming a completely self-sufficient homesteader is a tremendous amount of work. Imagine only eating food you grow yourself and using only products you make. We learned early on in our homesteading adventures that we would do what we could do, and what we couldn't do we would first look at supporting other homesteaders, farmers, and creatives in our area. If we couldn't find what we needed produced locally, we would search for it used or from a company with good ethics.

When deciding how you would like to be more self-sufficient, it is important to think about the desired space you would like to do that in. Food preservation, fermentation, cooking from scratch, making your own clothes, and growing microgreens do not require any land. Enough fruits and vegetables can be grown on a small piece of land to support an average-sized family. If you want to raise animals you will need more land (unless raising small animals like quail, rabbits, or chickens—these could all be done on a small scale in a standard-sized backyard). How much more would depend on how many and what kind of animals you plan to raise. Having a large piece of land can sound fantastic, but it can be a lot of work from the maintenance perspective (land clearing, fencing, mowing, etc.). Think about the exact activities you will want to do on your homestead and then figure out how much land you need to accomplish your goals. Some people love working with livestock, and some do not. Some people love spending lots of time cultivating food, and some do not. Do not romanticize things. Be honest with yourself about what you want to do and how much work it will be. Also, talking to other people who have done what

you want to do is an often-overlooked resource that can save time, energy, and money. If you do not know anyone doing what you would like to do, find people on social media and follow along with their journeys. Offer to volunteer at a farm or homestead with an operation you would aspire to, if possible. Like learning a new language, immersion in a particular environment is an incredibly effective way to learn new methods and skills. You can also listen to a podcast or read books. Do not dive in blindly. Learn as much as possible and make educated decisions. This will save much time and money.

Also consider climate. If the dream is an avocado grove, for example, New Hampshire is not the place. Either the dream or the location will need to be reworked. Certain plants and animals are best suited to particular climates or landscapes. Trying to grow a plant or raise a specific animal in a climate it is not well adapted for will be at best problematic and at worst a disastrous economic failure. So what is more important to you? The location of your homestead or what you plan to do on it?

SCALE

What scale do you want to work on? Is the goal to produce enough of something to be independent of outside sources or to be able to sell it to others?

Here is an example: a person enjoys making fiber art paintings and wants to pursue it as an income stream. They also want to make sure the wool they use is chemical-free and from animals that have been cared for humanely and as part of a regenerative grazing operation. They could pursue this on different scales in several different ways.

1. Find a local source for their wool. Visit farms in person and ask about the ethical and environmental impact they are making. Make sure the source is producing the wool in a way that meets their standards. Work out a monetary agreement based on cash payment or work trade; the work trade could be commissioned pieces of fiber art or perhaps help around the wool producer's farm if that was appealing to both parties.

2. Obtain a piece of land large enough for a small flock of sheep. They could produce all their own wool and probably even have extra to sell. They could even breed and sell a few sheep a year to contribute to the cost of paying for the land.

3. Buy a larger piece of land and raise a large herd of sheep, selling the excess wool and the lambs. It would be a good idea to have a distribution plan in place before committing to a project of this size.

These different scenarios can be applied to almost any crop or livestock situation, and often, people start on the "produce enough for my family and me" path before scaling up. Sometimes when people go the scenario number two route, they realize that whatever they are doing is a labor of love and are not interested in doing it on a larger scale. But as you can see, a person who wants an ethical source of wool could live in an apartment and still satisfy the desire to create beautiful fiber art.

Another scenario is that if you want to grow food just for your family, you can do that in a sub-urban-sized yard. If you are in an apartment, you should seek out a community garden in your area and if there isn't one, approach the city council with ideas for creating one. Gauge local interest. Can you get a hundred or a thousand signatures for converting an abandoned lot into a productive edible landscape? In the meantime, seek out people in your area who are growing food and buy directly from them via farmers markets, crop swaps, or social media. You can grow sprouts, microgreens, and herbs indoors until your dreams of a community garden and/or land ownership can be realized. Gourmet mushrooms can be grown in closets.

Once a vision and scale have been decided, access to land may be necessary. The land should be suitable for the desired crop(s) or purpose. Make sure to know the types of soil and climate conditions best suited for what you would like to produce. It is important to understand how water flows on and around the property: Where are the wet spots? Are there areas prone to flooding? What is the path of the sun? Are there other mitigating factors to consider, such as noise pollution from highways or neighbors, actual pollution from runoff, neighbors, or previous owners (soil and water tests should be done)? Are there any easements through the property that would hinder developing it the way you would like?

Also consider that if funds are a limiting factor, there may be a way to lease or use land owned by another person who does not have the time or interest to manage it. For example, someone may own a few acres of land that they have to pay to have mowed every year that they would be happy to have a few rotationally grazed sheep or cows on because it would allow them to save a few dollars while improving the soil.

When investing in land, it is good to know about the neighbors on the surrounding land. What are they producing? What do they put into the soil? Are they friendly? Following are questions you should consider as you develop your goals. I ask these same questions to clients in my consulting practice. If you are looking to homestead with a partner or a group of people, this should be discussed together so that everyone who is part of the decision-making process is on the same page.

HOW TO CHOOSE A LOCATION AND LAND

- Do I like to live in close community, or do I like to live a more solitary existence?
- Are there certain people I would like to stay geographically close to?
- Who are my neighbors?
    › Are they like-minded?
    › Does this matter in my particular case?
- Land questions:
    › Is the land suitable for what I want to do soil-wise and water-wise?
    › Soil test results:
    › Water test results:
    › Where is the access to water?
    › What watershed does the property belong to?
    › How does water flow onto and off of the property?
    › Is this property prone to flooding?

› What was this land used for in the last hundred years? Find out as far back as you can. Is there any possible contamination?

› Noise, air, visual, or other forms of pollution:

You might find that your homestead goals morph as you gain knowledge and experience. That is okay. Reassess every year or so to make sure your goals and vision align with your life. Be honest with yourself about who you are. If you are an extrovert who loves spending most of your time with others but you also have big dreams of living on a fully sustainable off-grid farm, you may want to seek out other like-minded individuals who would want to buy land with or near to you, so you don't end up lonely and bored on your awesome farm.

Do you have visions of yourself living on the land but lack inspiration about what you would like to produce? Following are some ideas. I suggest producing something that you use or buy fairly often; that is why raising chickens for eggs or growing a garden can be great first choices. I also suggest that anything added to the homestead should serve at least three different purposes. Examples of purposes could be food, shelter, nature crafting, wildlife habitat, fiber, beauty, joy, etc. If you cannot think of at least three reasons to bring a particular plant, animal, or hobby to your homestead, you may not want to do it. Also, many animals, plants, and hobbies can stack and help make each other more resilient. Here are some examples:

• Bees: honey, pollination for garden or orchard, wax for candles or personal care products
• Sheep: pasture management, wool (from wool varieties), manure to use in gardens, and raising extra sheep to sell as an income stream
• Flowers: beauty, habitat for pollinators, a possible income stream, pressed flowers for gift-giving
• Fruit tree: food, wildlife habitat, shade

Notice how the bees can work with fruit trees and flowers, and the sheep (if grazing was set up correctly) could help fertilize a fruit tree or orchard. It is fairly easy to come up with three reasons to have something on a homestead, which is why it is the minimum number for me. And be aware of how the different systems you are looking to create will impact each other. For example, if you want to raise livestock and have a vegetable garden or orchard, you will need good fencing so the goats don't destroy your hard work.

Once the homestead's scale, location, and production desires have been decided, it is a good idea to map where everything will go. I encourage you to print an aerial photo of your land and create overlays with tracing paper. Make a list of elements you would like on your homestead and create several layouts to decide what makes the most sense for your goals. Also, while planning, it is important to consider the things addressed earlier, such as access to water and the way water flows on your property, noise, and visual pollution, etc. In permaculture, we try to see "problems" as opportunities. If you wish to obstruct a view, maybe this would be a good place to plant some trees. A wet spot on a property could be turned into a pond that could also be used for irrigation in drier months. A section of seemingly overgrown, impassible woods, if properly fenced, could be used to graze pigs or goats, turning the overgrown woods into a monetary benefit and eventually clearing out the understory and opening it up to other opportunities such as mushroom cultivation.

Part of good stewardship is to observe and respond to the land, so if the original design needs to be tweaked a little (or a lot), then do so. And although it may not be a luxury everyone can afford, I strongly urge you to observe your property through four seasons before setting up major infrastructure that will be hard to change. Make notes and take account of the native flora and fauna before imposing your will on it; if you don't, you may miss some valuable feedback from your land, such as an area prone to flooding or a valuable plant that will only grow in the spring. Plant species will give clues to what land need. For example, bindweed can be an indicator of compacted soil while mullein can be pervasive in very alkaline soil.

CHAPTER 3

GARDENING FOR AN ABUNDANT FOOD SUPPLY

The food we choose to eat is one of the most powerful choices we make. Every bite we consume impacts our health, the environment, animals, and other humans.

Pesticides, herbicides, fungicides, and chemical fertilizers are pervasive in our food supply and soil, thanks to over a hundred years of chemical agriculture. Industrialized food systems have abused animals and people, polluted the environment, and dispensed products detrimental to human health.

Growing our own food is a health decision and it is an ethical one. It is also an issue of sustainability because the current model of centralized food systems uses a tremendous number of resources via packaging food and moving it from place to place. It produces an egregious amount of waste at the harvest and retail levels (there is much waste after food is purchased as well, but that is another topic).

The highest quality of food can be cost-prohibitive and hard to find. It is nearly impossible to do on a large scale and completely impossible on a centralized scale. These reasons led my family to begin growing fruits and vegetables and raising animals. We also support small regenerative farmers for what we cannot produce independently. There are ways to grow an abundant supply of food without having to wage war on nature or poison the soil and water supply.

In 1944, in the era of victory gardens, it was estimated that more than 40 percent of all of the fresh fruits and vegetables consumed in the United States were grown in backyards. Home gardening is seeing a resurgence, with an estimated one in three households growing edible foods today. Between home and community garden projects, there is no reason we could not meet and even exceed the percentage of food currently being grown with decentralized production methods.

GARDENING FOR AN ABUNDANT FOOD SUPPLY

RESEARCH NATIVES OR BIO REGIONALLY APPROPRIATE PLANTS

Before growing food in an area, do a bit of research about what will grow best in that climate. What used to grow wild, or maybe still does, in the uncultivated areas of the place?

Before industrial agriculture began monocropping a few handfuls of crops that transported across large distances well and had a long shelf life, there used to be all kinds of wild foods that grew, foods that were already adapted to a particular environment. In fact, many plants, a couple of generations ago, were a common food source that are now looked upon as weeds.

Dandelions used to be gathered to use in salads and soups and made into wine; now many people spray herbicides on these "weeds" or rip them out of their chemical-laden nonedible lawn. It is insanity if you think about it—someone disdainfully ripping a dandelion out of their yard to put it in a non-compostable plastic bag, then going to the market and buying salad greens in a plastic bag or container. We throw away free food and then go spend money on similar food that is packaged in a way that damages the environment. It is sort of mind-blowing how upside-down the thinking around food has become.

Anywhere people live, even in the desert of Arizona, there are edible plants. It is simply a matter of locating them, identifying them, and learning how to prepare them. So before creating a landscape design that is all wrong for a climate and contains zero plants that will contribute an edible yield, I urge people to figure out the plants that grow wild in their area and which ones are edible and incorporate them into the landscape design. I don't think there is any need to be a complete purist about using only edible plants, but once I begin researching a region for a design, there are plenty of plants with edible parts that most people believe to be entirely ornamental. Figuring out what will grow abundantly and easily in an area and then learning palatable ways to consume it will save much time and energy in the long run.

Pawpaws, black eyed peas, okra, and muscadines are all bioregionally
appropriate foods to grow in my area of the Southeast.

In home vegetable gardens, particular crops are often grown that may not be entirely suitable for the climate they are being grown in because they are the foods people have become accustomed to seeing in the grocery store. Carrots, tomatoes, potatoes, and peas will all grow better in some climates than others. It is okay to force these things if that is what you want to do. I know I certainly try to grow things not native to where I live; when talking about building resilience and growing as many things as we can as easily as possible, it is simply less labor-intensive to grow the food that thrives in our climate. For example, it is notoriously difficult to grow apple and peach trees where I live (without pesticides, herbicides, or fungicides, that is), and I still try because my family loves apples and peaches. But I am also trying to nurture some pawpaws into production because I know they can produce abundantly in my bioregion with little outside help once established. Most grapes have difficulty thriving in the high humidity of the southeast, which leads to fungal problems. But passion fruit and blackberries grow well. So I have a couple of grape varieties resistant to fungal diseases, and I am learning to utilize the fruits better adapted to my climate. These fruits will give me a greater yield with a fraction of the effort.

Gardening for a regenerative homestead and a holistic and sustainable lifestyle must see some sort of shift in the products that people demand availability of. The food system we have perpetuated is unsustainable partly because we have fallen in love with foods that don't grow anywhere near us, and a love for what will thrive in our environment has not been cultivated because the foods that would be pervasive if our environment was left wild might rot within a few days of harvest and don't look as pretty on a supermarket shelf. It is also learning and accepting what may be available in a particular season and not demanding uniformity of diet year-round.

Pawpaws are a good example of this. If you have ever had that banana pudding at holiday potlucks in the south, know that you are eating somewhat of a traditional dessert. However, because bananas do not thrive in that area but pawpaw used to, the dessert was traditionally made with pawpaws, which have a texture similar to bananas. Pawpaws do not store or ship well, so groves were cut down to plant apples, which require massive amounts of chemicals to produce and massive amounts of fuel to transport.

Plants considered invasive but also edible can often be controlled somewhat by figuring out edible or medicinal uses. An example of this where I live is the Bradford pear. Every year my daughters and I harvest baskets of the tiny fruit that is somewhat astringent if eaten out of hand and processed into syrup or jelly. This tree is frequently spread by wildlife consuming the fruit and then releasing the seeds elsewhere. By harvesting and using them, we keep these seeds from being planted. If more people used the fruit, maybe the species could be better controlled. Are there species that are considered "invasive" where you live? Do some research and see what these plants could be used for. I do not bring up invasive plants as an encouragement to plant them but to point out ways to control things beyond poisoning them.

Gardeners should be aware that growing all the foods they grew up on will be more work than staying within the bounds of what nature can do so easily and effectively when it is simply cooperated with. The environment can be a supremely abundant place! Especially when it has our support.

PLANNING A GARDEN

Choosing a site

A good way to put together a design for a space is to create a site map that is an aerial view of the property. This can be done by hand or using a program like Google Earth to get a satellite image. Then use tracing paper to draw by hand or a computer program like PowerPoint to create overlays of the site with information and design ideas. There are many wonderful books on this topic.

Flowers in a garden are for more than aesthetics; they provide a food source for pollinators,
so they will help increase yields, and tiny birds, which will help keep insect populations in check.

SITE ZONES

When designing, also pay attention to zones. (This is not referring to hardiness zones.) The zone refers to how frequently a part of the property is visited. The elements a person would visit most often should be the closest, while the parts of a design that need visiting weekly, monthly, or seasonally should be farther away. For example, the herb garden might be in zone 1, the veggie garden in zone 2, and the berry bushes or fruit trees in zones 3 or 4. There should also, if possible, be a zone 5. This is an area that is not used for production but left wilder; this is helpful for observation and provides habitat for native flora and fauna.

WATER

When planning to grow anything, make sure the location has good drainage and access to a sustainable water source. Using a rainwater catch is an amazing way to utilize water that simply runs off buildings. It can be stored in tanks with a first flush diverter so that the water is not contaminated by things built up on the roof.

The calculation for determining the amount of water that can be collected from the roof of a structure is:

- Length of roof: _____ feet times width of roof: _____ feet = X
- X times the amount of rainfall in inches = Y
- Y x .623 = _____ gallons of rainfall collected

This will be useful in determining the necessary size of a rainwater collection receptacle and it can also be used to figure out how much rainwater can be harvested from a particular site annually. Most rain events are one inch or less. The number of inches of rain in a location varies widely but can be easily researched. Rainwater catch is not legal in all areas, so check with your extension office or the regulatory body in your area.

A pond can also be dug on a high point of the property and then channeled downhill (through horizontal rather than vertical channels to reduce erosion), watering gardens and orchards on the way. This is also referred to as terracing. Berms are used when the slopes are less drastic, but the idea is the same: slow the flow of water on a property to create as much absorption and the least amount of runoff. The ground itself can act as a water tank; the more organic matter in the soil, the more the ground will act as a sponge. Mulching gardens and orchards with organic materials or even using living mulches (groundcover) is a good way to slow the evaporation of the water from the soil back into the atmosphere.

SUN

Most food plants need at least six hours of sun a day to produce a good yield. Some plants will produce in the shade or partial shade. But if choosing a space for a traditional vegetable garden, six hours or more of sun a day is a requirement.

HARDINESS ZONES

Knowing your hardiness zone is important because it is tied to regional frost dates. Make sure not to set out tender young plants before the last frost in spring and cover them or protect them in fall. Pay attention to this when purchasing perennials. Depending on how cold a region gets, some plants can survive through winter and be perennial, while others would only last one year. Establishing perennials will help to maximize your time, energy, and finances. Finding out the zone of a particular area is easy. I like to use the Farmer's Almanac website.

CHILL HOURS

Knowing the typical number of chill hours in a region and matching that to appropriate cultivars of fruit trees is important. It will help to avoid poor fruit sets.

SOIL HEALTH

Soil is alive. There are millions of microbes with jobs to do and we should do our best to avoid tilling soils as this effectively kills the soil life. These microbes are essential for helping plants uptake moisture and nutrients, similar to how the gut microbiome helps food digest properly. When gut health is poor, people can eat healthy and still be malnourished because the body cannot effectively absorb what it needs. Poor soil health means there will have to be a massive number of inputs into a growing space and the plants will not be able to utilize the nutrients effectively, creating much more work for the gardener. When building a garden, the importance of building healthy soils cannot be overstated!

To create beds ready to plant in, try layering organic matter like cardboard, wood chips, straw, or hay that has not gone to seed, animal manure, grass clippings, vegetable scraps, compost, leaves, etc. (Cardboard is good for smothering grass but must be given four to six months or so to break down before being planted in, so skip this step if trying to plant right away. I use it when building beds in fall that will be planted the following spring.) Make sure to have an even amount of green or wet ingredients or dry or brown ingredients so there is a balance in place. Too many green ingredients will be a soupy, stinky mess, and too much brown will also be trouble. Do a few inches of each layer in the fall, and then plant in the spring. If the layers are placed and planted too quickly, it will not have the desired outcome because the pile will probably start to compost and get hot while the plants are in it, and they could be killed. When creating a new garden bed to plant in right away, use a mix of topsoil and compost topped with no more than four inches of wood chips. Also, wood chips can be raked back in subsequent seasons to plant or add compost and then raked back when plants have sprouted or are established. Avoid stirring wood chips into soil as they will pull nitrogen from soil as they break down. Note that the method of layering cardboard is not advisable around a young, just-planted tree unless often artificially irrigated. Instead, use a thick layer of compost or wood chips and plant companion plants around trees.

Soil health can also be enhanced with proper livestock. Ruminants can be grazed rotationally to increase fertility and topsoil. Chickens and pigs can clear, prep, and aerate soil. We often move our mobile chicken coop to areas we want to plant and leave the chickens in place for a few days to clear the area. When livestock is rotated and moved to fresh pasture regularly, they are healthier because this breaks the lifecycle of parasites. Excess manure can be harvested and added to gardens.

Rotational grazing is a beneficial practice because it keeps pastures and grasslands from being over-grazed and it also keeps the parasite levels in the grazing animals lower. Lower parasite levels will lead to better health and body conditions for the animals and reduce or eliminate the need for chemical de-wormers. Animals can be rotated in many ways. The animals can be moved at least every sixth day (some farmers move their animals daily to ensure maximum uptake of forage and weight gain, four to six days to stay ahead of the parasite lifecycle of about six days). Parasites can live dormant for about 120 days. Another way to approach this, if you cannot move the animals as often or have to move them through fewer paddocks, would be to never let the grass get shorter than four inches or so, as parasites will live on the lowest two inches of the grass.

Multispecies grazing also helps break the parasite cycle. An example is grazing cattle with sheep and goats. This is because these parasites do not typically impact the cattle. Following cows with chickens is also helpful, as they will break up the manure and eat some of the larvae. You could also graze all the animals together in the same paddock. The paddocks can be broken up by permanent fencing, high tensile electric, electro net, or, over a longer term, living hedgerows can be integrated (for cattle) because they make good fence and forage. Planting trees along fence lines can be a good long-term strategy when rotationally grazing. Plant trees that are good animal forage/feed. Plant far enough from the fence line to protect the tree from grazing while young. In time, the tree will act as feed and shade for livestock while controlling erosion. Rotational grazing can be done in different ways with different forages, species, fence types, time in paddocks, and rest periods. The key is to mimic the natural way a herd or flock of animals in the wild would come through an area to graze and move on to a new area when they have eaten the favored forage. See the resources section for more recommendations.

Having animals as a part of the ecosystem is important. Much of the food grown today requires large amounts of petroleum-based fertilizers to produce, while animal waste products from confinement feeding operations that are not properly utilized will cause pollution. Animals, and their waste products, are all a part of a healthy and natural ecosystem.

COMPANION PLANTING

Let's talk about companion planting. In nature, we never find a whole mass of one thing with no other plants. Different plants live together harmoniously in symbiotic relationships. Gardeners can attempt to recreate this in edible landscapes, orchards, or food forests. Many books give in-depth information on how to do this. I encourage you to read more on food forestry and permaculture if growing food is something you are interested in doing. The gist of it, however, is that it is always better to plant more than one type of plant in each area. Planting a large area with one type of crop makes that crop vulnerable to disease and pest predation. Planting veggie beds with several varieties intercropped together will confuse pests. Growing several varieties of tomatoes instead of one reduces the likelihood of a disease that will wipe out the entire crop. In nature, diversity equals resilience. I like to plant vegetable beds with different crops that I know play well together. I also like to plant garlic, chives, nasturtium, and marigolds at the head and foot of my veggie beds and zinnias (or another flower that attracts pollinators and small birds) throughout. Many pests will be repelled by the scent of garlic, chives, marigolds, and nasturtium. Pollinators will help increase your yields, and small birds will eat pests in the garden and be a feast for the eyes. When planting a garden, think about it not just as growing a few veggies or flowers but as creating an ecosystem.

We like to plant garlic in our vegetable beds and around fruit trees as a pest repellant.

WHAT IS PERMACULTURE?

Permaculture is a way of approaching design in which we work in cooperation with the given environment rather than against it. It is mostly used to describe a form of agriculture, but the twelve principles it is based on can be applied to any design. As far as I know, permaculture is the only type of gardening with a set of ethics. Bill Mollison and David Holmgren coined the term *permaculture* in the 1970s. The word itself is a combination of the words "permanent" and "agriculture," and with its focus on perennials rather than annuals, like the current agricultural model, it would be easy to sum it up as food growing with a concentration on perennials. But that would not be doing justice to the potentially revolutionary permaculture system. The central ethics, in order, are:

- Design for the earth.
- Design for yourself (people).
- Create a surplus (that can be shared).

The principles are as follows:

1. Observe and Interact

Spend some time at the site you will be designing. Understand the weather patterns, how the water moves on the site, and microclimates. Where does the sun hit the property? Where is there shade? Is there a noise problem? A view that should be protected or blocked? When designing with permaculture, there is no such thing as a one-size-fits-all approach. The design is as unique as the property and the people it is being created for.

2. Catch and Store Energy

We know sun is energy. But some people think the only way to catch the sun and store its energy would be solar panels attached to a battery. There are many ways to capture the sun's energy, like grass or a vegetable garden. Grass is energy for livestock and vegetables are energy for humans.

What about water barrels in a greenhouse that can collect heat during the day and release it at night to keep plants warm? What about capturing the energy of a flowing stream with a water turbine and using it to power a pump? The possibilities are limitless. There are many energy sources all around us and even more ways to store it.

3. Obtain a Yield

Beauty can be a yield. But, unless it is your absolute favorite plant ever, it should also serve another purpose. When thinking about how to landscape a home, there is absolutely no reason why most plants should not be edible. Many ornamentals are also entirely or partially edible (daylilies, roses, or violets, to name a few). If you have a favorite type of fruit or vegetable that grows in your climate, figure out how to grow it. Get rewarded for all of your hard work! When I place an element into a design, I like to see that it serves at least three purposes. For example: It is beautiful, edible, and a pollinator habitat. Or it is shade, nitrogen-fixing, and provides forage for my chickens. I do this when obtaining animals for our farm (for chickens: eggs, bug control, manure; for Angora rabbits: fiber, companionship, manure). If something does not serve at least three different purposes, I feel like I could make a better choice.

4. Apply Self-Regulation and Accept Feedback

Pay attention to the systems you have put in place and make necessary adjustments and improvements. Sometimes a need to be right can prevent us from seeing a situation for what it is and prevent us from taking steps to create true success. Be honest about what is working and not working and be open to feedback from the environment and people. Also, when choosing plants for an environment, make sure to consider what they will be when they reach their full size.

5. Use Renewable Resources

Some resources, like oil, for example, are not renewable. Others are, especially when managed properly. Using wood for heat in an efficient wood stove with proper forestry management ensures that there will be a never-ending supply of wood to use as heat. Adding shade around a home and positioning it in such a way to protect it from the extreme midday heat in summer can reduce the need for artificial climate control and reduce the amount of energy needed to keep it comfortable for the inhabitants. A pecan tree can be used for shade, food, wood, and eventually heat or compost. More can be planted. Trees are an awesome example of a renewable resource.

6. Produce No Waste

What a radical idea today. No waste? Most households in the US fill up one of those giant flip-top garbage cans every week. That doesn't include the large items of furniture or appliances that get taken to the dump. How many people take completely biodegradable food scraps and put them in a non-biodegradable plastic bag that will be placed in a landfill and still be there when the person who created that garbage is no longer on the planet?

Meanwhile, the topsoil in our country has been much reduced in the last couple of hundred years (thanks to deforestation and erosion), and the soil that is left is nutrient-poor. The food we grow can only be as nutrient-dense as the soil it is grown in. So how about returning the nutrients to soil through composting? It is not difficult; it's finding a system that works for you and implementing it.

Some people like to manually turn their compost or have worm farms or big bins they keep it in, which can be turned with a handle. We like a put-it-and-forget-it system. We have a three-bin system that we constructed out of old pallets we got for free. By the time we fill up the third bin, the compost in the first bin is broken down and ready for use. The leaves that get bagged up and thrown away? These make an excellent mulch to put on your garden beds in the winter or add to your compost.

If you have no use for your compost—for example, if you live in an apartment and have no plants— consider reaching out to your community to see if anyone would want your food waste so they can compost it; a small local farm might be a good option. Also a few chickens are excellent for turning household food waste into delicious eggs.

7. Design from Patterns to Details

Many patterns are repeated in nature that you can mimic in your designs: a spiral, the veins in a leaf, a wave, etc. These patterns occur naturally again and again because they work and are functional. Observe them and notice where they would be appropriate in a design.

8. Integrate Rather than Segregate

In many agricultural models today, there is a mono-crop system. Acres of corn or soybeans. A huge orchard with one kind of tree. The thought process is that if there is one kind of plant, it will all be easier to manage and maintain. The soil becomes depleted and creates an environment in which a particular pest species can proliferate in an unchecked way because it has an unlimited food supply. When observing how plants naturally occur, we notice there are never acres and acres of one plant and nothing else. In permaculture, we plant groups of plants together. A heavy feeding fruit tree would get planted with a nitrogen-fixing plant to put nitrogen back in the soil, pollinator plants to attract bees and butterflies, pest-deterring plants like nasturtium or garlic, a ring of daffodils to suppress grass growth, and a dynamic accumulator species like comfrey or coneflower that pulls nutrients from soil and can be chopped and used as mulch to feed the tree. Instead of chemical fertilizers and pesticides, we can benefit from the intelligence of natural systems.

9. Use Small and Slow Solutions

When people begin to grow their own food, sometimes they can be turned off by the amount of time perennial crops can take to produce. They want food now, or in a few months, at the most. And that is okay. I love some of the annual vegetables. But make the same investment of time and money into a perennial crop, like an asparagus bed, a berry bush, or a nut or fruit tree, and in a few years, there will be an established crop that will yield year after year with little input. It can be hard to wait but worth it. And if you plant several trees that bear fruit and nuts, many berry bushes, and crops like artichokes and asparagus, in a few years, the reliance on the annual crops will be reduced and so will the amount of energy spent gardening.

10. Use and Value Diversity

Diversity is important when growing food because planting all of any crop makes it more vulnerable to attack by disease and predators. For example, instead of planting ten fruit trees that are all one or two types of apple, plant three apples, a couple of pears, a couple of stone fruits like peaches or cherries, and a couple of jujubes or pawpaws. Ensure you have the correct number and type of pollinators for the trees, but get as many varieties as possible. That way, if it is a bad apple year because of weather, pests, or another variable, hopefully a few of the other fruit trees do well. This is true in the annual garden as well. Plant different varieties of squash, melons, and tomatoes. You will find that some of them do better in your climate, are lower maintenance, and are more resistant to predators. Consulting a local nursery that specializes in varieties that thrive in your region when selecting perennials is a good idea.

11. Use the Edges

The "edges" are where two spaces meet and they can be areas with many possibilities. The area where the yard meets the woods or the grass meets the pond, for example, can create a microclimate that might be perfect for cultivating a certain crop that does not exist anywhere else on the property.

Also consider the shape of the garden beds; the keyhole bed is a popular shape in permaculture because it maximizes growing space and minimizes path space. Realize anywhere a little different on a site has its own microclimate and possibilities. Example: A shed with a wall that gets half-sun/half-shade with a roof that's angled in the same direction, so it also gets rainwater. This could be a great spot to plant something like elderberry.

12. Creatively Use and Respond to Change

Understand that no two years will be exactly alike. Keep a notebook and practice bringing it along when harvesting fruit and vegetables or doing maintenance. Take notes and create informed courses of action.

WHAT IS A GUILD?

A plant guild is a cooperative supercharged team of plants that work together to create maximum vitality and yields. Have you ever gone for a walk in the woods? Is there just one type of tree with no other plants? No. There are usually several kinds of trees, maybe some shrubs, an herb layer, a few mushrooms, and vines. These plants are all working together symbiotically. This means they will have more protection from pests and disease and require less input from you.

If you have never heard of a plant guild, the concept may seem overwhelming, but it is not complicated. If we can model our systems on those in nature, we will not have to rely on chemical fertilizers and pesticides to grow our food.

The layers of a plant guild

These are the layers you can place into your guild, followed by some examples of plants that make up those layers to give you some ideas.

- **Tall tree layer**: pecan, conifer, full-size fruit tree
- **Shorter tree layer**: semi-dwarf fruit tree
- **Shrub/bush**: blueberry, blackberry, currant
- **Herb**: comfrey, basil, milkweed
- **Ground cover**: strawberry, thyme
- **Root**: sweet potato, garlic
- **Vine**: grape, wisteria, passionflower. Keep in mind with this layer that a vine will need a large tree to climb; a grapevine could overcome a young, semi-dwarf apple tree but would be fine growing on your larger tree layer. You could also incorporate a trellis for your vine or perhaps head-train them nearby.
- You can also include a **fungi** or **mushroom** layer.

Different functions within a guild

- **Fruiting plants** produce an edible yield. Nut and fruit trees and berries fill this function. You can also incorporate perennial vegetables into your guild, like artichokes and asparagus.
- **Nitrogen fixers** help add nitrogen to the soil so that the plants have more of this important element that contributes to healthy growth. Some good nitrogen fixers: black locust, Siberian pea shrub, goumi berry, wisteria, clover, and lupine.
- **Insectary species** are plants attract beneficial insects and birds. Keep in mind almost anything that flowers will do this, but some do it better than others. The key is to have different things flowering at different times of year so there is always food for beneficial insects and birds, so they stay around to keep pest species in check. Insects pollinate and some are also predatory, and birds help keep the pest insect populations

from exploding: peppermint (but this can be invasive), pineapple sage, dill, zinnias, and yarrow.

- **Repellants** are plants have smells pests don't like and protect them from invasion. Garlic, chives (any allium, really), thyme, nasturtium, marigold, and tarragon are good pest-deterring plants.
- **Accumulators** are plants accumulate nutrients in their foliage and can be cut down and used as mulch for heavier feeders. When they die back in winter, it is thought that the foliage and taproots release nutrients back into the soil. Comfrey, coneflower, yarrow, and mullein are some examples.
- **Weed suppressors** include examples like daffodils planted in a ring around your tree help to suppress the grass, or strawberries acting as ground cover. Mulch can suppress weeds and break down to add organic matter to soil.

Look at this explanation for the plant guild on page 80. See how some plants fill more than one function. When planting anything it is a good idea to research that plant in several sources. Also consider talking to a local expert, like an orchardist, a nursery worker, or someone at a nearby botanical garden to ask how this plant may perform in the area.

Consider thinking outside of the box. Instead of an apple tree, maybe a jujube tree or a pawpaw could be a good fit. In my experience, most fruit trees produced in a massive commercial context have more problems with pests and disease. Is it a coincidence that apples are one of the most widely grown fruit crops and one of the most susceptible to pests and disease? There are many food plants that we do not encounter in our modern society because their products do not store or ship well. Pawpaws, mulberries, elderberries, passion fruits, currants, and the like are all delicious and full of nutrition, but they are too delicate to withstand the collection methods and shipping that the modern food systems require of its products.

Think of any particular nuisance a plant could create as well. For example, a fruiting mulberry could be a great addition to your landscape, but placing it where people walk daily may result in the fruit finding its way onto their shoes and making stains on the floors of your home. Perhaps place it on the edge of your yard where it warrants a special trip so that fruit traveling into your home on the bottoms of people's shoes is less likely.

The possibilities are endless! Make a list of some favorite things to grow and eat and see if these can be combined into a guild. Also, I recommend against growing a plant you don't care for so it can fulfill a function. Do more research and find a plant you like that can play that part. You can also grow annual vegetables and roots under your tree layer while the tree is small because plenty of sun will still reach under the canopy.

Create more than one guild and plant a food forest. Some innovative farmers are planting fruit tree guilds with an "alley crop" in between, planted with annual crops while the fruit trees are young and the shade canopy has not filled in. Referring back to earlier in the chapter, I encourage you to design guilds with plants with a track record of being easy to grow in your area.

I am in zone 7a. Here is a sample of a guild that would work well in my area: Pecan tree (not depicted in diagram; overstory), two pawpaws (understory), Muscadine and passionflower (vine), mullein (accumulator), strawberry (suppressor), yarrow (insectary), shiitake logs (fungi), lupine (nitrogen fixer), daffodils (weed suppressor), garlic in a ring around fruit tree (repellant).

Research plants that are friendly to your area and thrive in your climate. Where I live in the Southeast it is difficult to grow peaches and grapes without chemicals because of the higher humidity levels, making these crops susceptible to fungus. I still grow them, but I take care to find resistant varieties, plant in an area with plenty of airflow, and honestly, I have to babysit them more than some of the other food crops I grow. I plant my peaches close to my house, where I can keep an eye on them and give them more TLC.

Fruit Tree Guild

Paw paw

Passion flower vine

Muscadine

Lupine
(nitrogen fixer)

Mullein
(dynamic accumulator)

Yarrow
(insectary)

Garlic
(repellent)

Shiitake

Daffodils & Strawberries
(weed suppression)

Example of a fruit tree guild

Sharing/selling/trading what you grow

Have you heard of an app called Cropswap? It is specifically geared toward small local producers of food. So if you produce more food than you can eat or preserve yourself, there is potential for you to be able to trade with neighbors. There are other apps and websites that I know are currently under development. Seeking out other gardening and farming friends to buy and trade with is a good idea. Our family also likes to gift some of what we grow; it is fun to share with friends and neighbors and it may just inspire them to plant their own garden. Loconomy.org is another great website useful for locating or listing small businesses. Social media and Craigslist are ways to connect with people locally. Investigate farmers markets, flea markets, and consignment shops in your town.

GROWING FOOD WITHOUT CHEMICALS

We don't use pesticides, not even organic ones, on our farm. We plant things in guilds, use companion planting in our annual vegetable garden, and get out there and pick off bugs by hand. We have chickens, guinea hens, and ducks to help control pests. We compost our food waste and spread it in the food gardens. And yes, we lose a little of our yield to bugs, birds, or squirrels. I would say on average 10 to 30 percent. I am okay with this. I consider it a tithe. The earth, insects, and wildlife are involved in a complex dance that I don't fully understand. I choose to work in harmony with it as much as possible and I believe that means giving back a little. Be proactive by knowing what pest and ally species look like (in all their different stages), so they can be removed or left alone when spotted, and put up a fence around the garden.

The idea that poison can be put on crops to kill pests and has no negative impact on beneficial microbes and insects, or on humans, is false. It is like the discovery that is being made now about antibiotics and the effect they have on the human biome. They take out the bad guys, but they take out a lot of good guys in the process. It is impossible to apply pesticides to soil and kill only the bad guys. Avoiding pesticides and herbicides is one of the main reasons I started growing food. Then I discovered how much better it tastes and how rewarding it feels. Growing fruit, nuts, and perennial vegetables and herbs is much less labor-intensive than growing all of your food with annuals.

Tend to the soil

The importance of soil health cannot be overstated. Compost that is free from any chemical residue is a must (for example, conventional vegetable and fruit scraps that are saturated with pesticides and fungicides). Composted chicken, cow, or horse manure are also good. Keep in mind that if animals are fed GMO grains, or given chemical wormers and antibiotics, those compounds will be in their manure and make their way into your soil, food, and body. Blood meal, bone meal, worm castings, and liquid kelp are other excellent ways to amend your soil. I like to find weeds with deep roots that have not yet gone to seed, like dandelion, comfrey, mullein, thistle, or nettle (which is also great—even though it doesn't have a deep taproot, it is still mineral-rich). These can be dried outside until crispy and then ground up and sprinkled back onto your soil or brewed into a "tea" and then diluted and used as liquid fertilizer. The brew will be stinky but effective.

ABOUT TILLING

Try not to till if possible. Why not? Tilling soil kills the microbes. It was explained to me once like this: Tilling soil is like if a disaster came through a city and destroyed it, and it had to be rebuilt. Yearly tilling essentially kills most of your soil life on an annual basis. Healthy soil will have millions of microorganisms per square foot and tilling it will kill these organisms, leaving it to try to rebuild itself. Also, healthy soil is extremely effective at sequestering carbon, whereas tilling releases massive amounts of carbon into the atmosphere. If you have to till to prep the garden initially, avoid doing it yearly. A good way to prep an area for planting is to lay cardboard or layers of newspaper down in the shape of your garden space and then add layers of organic material that will break down and create beautiful soil. We will also temporarily place chicken coops on areas we would like to prepare for gardening as they will scratch and dig out many weeds while adding manure. We then add the compost, soil, and mulch layers.

The tobacco hornworm can defoliate certain crops quickly, causing major damage. It is the caterpillar of the Carolina Sphinx moth. Certain pollinators co-evolve with certain plant species and we are not currently aware of all these relationships. I encourage you to learn about insects you perceive as garden pests and their role in the ecosystem in all their phases.

I THOUGHT THIS SECTION WAS ABOUT PEST CONTROL...

It is! And we are getting there. Like a healthy body that gets proper nutrition will be better at protecting itself from disease and recovering from illness, healthy plants are less vulnerable to pests and disease. The only way to get truly healthy plants is through healthy soil. And it all comes full circle because for our bodies to be truly healthy, we must eat food grown in healthy soil. The nutrient content of certain fruits and vegetables has decreased over the last few generations because fewer vitamins and minerals are in the soil. And soil that is tilled regularly does not have the life present to extract the nutrients from the soil to the plants.

COMPOSTING

Many humans bag up fruit and veggie scraps in plastic and send them to a landfill and then put chemical fertilizers on the ground to make the food grow. This is clearly a broken system. So compost instead of trashing things and turn "garbage" into healthy soil that will grow healthy food that will grow healthy bodies. Here is a list of things that can be composted: Fruit and veggie scraps, lint, any organic material from your dustpan, uncoated cardboard, tea, coffee, eggshells (although some people rinse them first), grass clippings, weeds that have not yet gone to seed (burn the ones that have gone to seed using fire-safe techniques such as controlled burns with the supervision of the local fire department), leaves, pine needles, seed-free straw, uncoated paper plates, and more. Don't put things into the compost that are man-made, like plastic. Also, meat will get smelly (and possibly attract scavenger animals) and bones take too long to break down. Bones can be boiled to make broth and the remainder can get ground into a powder and sprinkled on the garden (bone meal).

THE MANY USES OF EGGSHELLS

Eggshells can be saved and used several ways. You can definitely keep it simple and throw them into your compost, but here are some other ways to use them: first, I always rinse them and keep them in a container or bowl while I collect them so they do not develop a bad odor.

- They can be smashed into small rough pieces and sprinkled around plants to keep slugs at bay.
- They make adorable zero-waste containers for seed starting. When I transplant, I gently crack the bottom so the roots can escape.
- Poke a hole at each end of the egg with a skewer and blow the contents out. Then boil the shells in salty water. These can be used for decoration; they can be painted, dyed, Modge-Podged, or simply kept as they are.
- For the following applications I also sanitize them further by putting them into the oven at 250°F for about a half-hour.
  › The eggshells can then be ground into a powder and fed back to chickens.
  › Put the powder in capsules and take them as supplements.
  › Add the powder to soup, smoothie, or bread recipes.
  › The powder can even be used to brush teeth or as an ingredient in homemade tooth powder.

Now for the pests

There are many different ways to control insect pests in the garden. Here are things I have done and had success with. Let me open this section with this thought: I do not ever expect to be able to eat 100 percent of my vegetable or fruit crops. I always overplant. We pay taxes at the store and taxes out of our paychecks; I expect anywhere from 10 to 30 percent of the food I grow to go back to the land in one way or another. Be it insects, birds, bunnies, deer, or a freak hailstorm in June. Call it a tax; call it a tithe. I use the sun, rain, pollinators, and microbes in the soil. These natural systems are enabling me to grow food. Humans are willing to pay the price for food at the store but expect to use everything nature can provide for free; we say, "No, that's *my* food. I grew that." But the truth is, we don't do it by ourselves, even though growing things can be hard work at times. Nature is our partner, and partners deserve a cut.

Almost every year, creatures in nature have taken some of my crops. Or due to varying weather I may have a bumper crop of peas, for example, but the tomatoes didn't do as well that year. By planting many things and looking at everything in nature as a partner and not an adversary, we will feel less disheartened. I am not saying invite all the neighborhood deer over for a party to eat the whole garden, because they will if given a chance, and it is okay to protect ourselves from obvious threats, the same way we would in a business transaction. But, if a sneaky one gets a few lettuces, it is not the end of the world.

A holistic approach to pest control that can be used in any situation. Ask yourself these questions:

When I have an insect or a critter that is becoming an issue, the first questions I have are:

1. What does that critter eat?

2. What eats the critter?

3. Is there anything that repels the critter?

Then you can decide if you should:

A. Introduce a predator.

B. Cut off its food source.

C. Use a plant or herb as a repellant.

D.   Create a barrier with a fence, row cover, or netting.

E.   All of the above.

You should also ask yourself, is this critter really a problem? Are they going to munch a few leaves and be gone? Or will they decimate the crop? Remember that every "pest" is part of the food chain. Obtaining a balance, not completely vanquishing every insect or problematic animal, should be the objective. Often, a certain pest will apply pressure for a certain time in the season and then nature will balance it out.

An example: One year we had a pill bug problem. Yes, pill bugs. I had never considered them a pest before (more of an ally because they can be used to entertain a toddler). But one year they came out in record numbers and devoured our tiny seedlings. We researched pill bug predators and found that toads were one, and one that we had already seen in our garden because they like to hide in the deep wood chip mulch. After learning more about the accommodations that toads prefer, we made the areas of the yard and garden where we had seen the highest number of pill bugs more toad friendly by adding a shallow pan of water with a few rocks in it (pollinators also love these) and turning a terracotta pot upside-down for the toad to use as a shelter. (We used a hammer to smash a toad-sized opening out of the side of the pot and then used some air-dried clay to mold around the jagged edges.) Decorating the pot can be a fun project for kids. They also sell adorable readymade toad houses. We also put a few smooth rocks on the ground near the pot and inside of it for bugs to hide and the toad to eat. Within a couple of weeks of setting up the toad houses, we found that there were still a few pill bugs, but not the massive numbers we had seen before. The bonus of this system is that the toads are not just eating pill bugs; they are eating many different bugs. You can come up with solutions like this for any pest problem. It is as simple as basic addition or subtraction. Pest + predator = fewer pests. Pests - food supply = fewer pests. It is so simple, and better than putting poison into the ground. That poison will find its way into the water supply, kill wildlife, and destroy the microbial diversity of the soil. The poison glyphosate is so prevalent in our environment now because of its widespread agricultural use that it can be found in measurable amounts in our rainwater.

Observation is also important. Your pest problems will vary from year to year, and truly, from month to month, based on weather and other variables. Spending time in your garden every day and looking at the plants up close is key to catching a problem before it gets out of control.

DEER

They can jump high, love vegetable gardens, and will eat a young fruit tree right up. Here are some ways to keep them out of your garden:

- **An eight-foot-high fence.** Deer-proof fencing is the most expensive and labor-intensive solution. If you have the resources and want to, this is your most deer-proof option.
- **A barrier using fishing line.** Pound four-foot T-posts into the corners of your garden, then use a fishing line to wrap around the T-posts at about the height of a deer's chest. The theory is that they cannot see it, but when they try to move in to use your garden as a buffet, they feel the fishing line on their chests, and it weirds them out, so they leave.
- **A dog.** This has proven most effective for us; the caveat is that it must be a dog that spends a majority of its time outside. We have a Great Pyrenees in our barnyard and a heeler in the yard of our home and both do a great job of letting deer know they are not welcome. (Although I did see a deer chasing the heeler one time—not sure what that was about.) The bonus is they keep predators away from our animals too.
- **Mark your territory.** Apparently, peeing around the perimeter of your garden may keep deer away, alerting them humans are in the area. Make sure you do not do this in view of your neighbors, as it may not be appreciated.
- **Motion-activated sprinkler.** So much potential for comic entertainment with a motion-activated sprinkler. I am almost positive that if I used this option, I would be getting sprayed way more often than the deer. If you are good at remembering things, like when to turn the motion-activated sprinkler off, then this could be a great option for you.

SQUASH BUGS, VINE BORERS, HORNWORMS, AND OTHER "BAD BUGS"

Keep an eye out. These are the worst garden baddies because they have the propensity to take out a crop relatively quickly. This is where observation becomes a powerful tool. If you don't go into the garden and look at the leaves for a week or two, that is enough time for the squash bug numbers to have exploded or the hornworms to have defoliated the tomatoes. (And peppers, we found out one year.) Make sure to be in the garden at least every few days, checking the underside of leaves. I like to carry a bucket of water and drop all the pests into it, and then dump it out for my chickens to feast on. If you see yellow or brown leaves on a plant or droppings on a leaf, investigate. Look on the underside of all the leaves of a plant. I also sometimes use a trick of dumping out a full bucket of water right around the plant's stem where it is coming out of the ground. This will sometimes make them come running out, trying to avoid the flood. Then I scoop them up and drop them in my bucket. Or squish them. A note on hornworms: these worms that can defoliate plants in just hours are the caterpillar of the five-spotted hawkmoth. Sometimes I collect the hornworms and put them far away from the garden on an extra "sacrifice tomato" that I plant so they can complete their lifecycle. People plant milkweed for monarchs. Why not an extra tomato for hawkmoths?

If they like being in the garden, enlist the help of children. I have five daughters, three of whom are old enough to be legitimate garden helpers. Something I have found to be effective over the years is enlisting them as bug catchers. I show them pictures from the internet or field guides of the bad insects in all their incarnations (egg, larvae or juvenile, adults), I explain what they damage in a garden, and I send them on their way. I have also, at times, given them a sort of uniform with a bucket of water, a net, and a little homemade flipbook with pictures of their targets printed and pasted onto notecards and then hole-punched and placed on a metal ring. That can be put on a string and then they have their little bad bug guide necklace at their fingertips if they get confused. I think it also makes them feel official.

Their little eyes are so focused, and they have a different vantage point than us. They are the perfect helpers for this task because children are so good at seeing what adult eyes miss. I also show them to look for droppings; this is especially helpful with spotting hornworms. When they are done collecting, we feed them to our chickens or guinea hens, far away from the garden. This isn't something I would ever force them to do because ultimately, I want my children to love the garden and have fond memories of it, so they want to continue to grow food when they are older.

Try to go out or have someone go out and bug pick at least once a week during garden season. Also, whether you are bug-picking yourself or have little helpers, picking early in the morning or an hour or two before dusk is best. More insects are active at those times, and the weather is not stifling. We want the next generation of earth stewards to have pleasant memories of garden tasks and the outdoors.

Plant resistant varieties and use trap crops. This applies to the squash, as I have not yet come across hornworm-resistant tomatoes. I have had great luck with rampicante squash, Tahitian melon squash, delicata, and luffa. Cucurbita moschata (also sometimes listed as c. moschata) are known to be resistant to vine borers and squash bugs because of their vigorous and thick vines. A great way to find resistant varieties that work well in your area is to ask other gardeners, which brings me to my next tip:

Stay connected. Find a local gardening group (or two, or three) in your area. This is the best place to gain regional gardening knowledge. You can connect with other gardeners (some of whom are master gardeners, or permaculturists, or have gardened for forty years, etc.) to ask questions and get inspiration. One of my favorite things is that it gives me a heads up on bad bugs. When I start seeing posts about a particular pest, I get out into my garden, and nine times out of ten, there they are. But without the reminder to keep an eye out for them, they could have easily done more damage. These online gardening groups are also great for organizing real-life meetups and seed swaps.

Leave the wasps alone. Yes, having wasps build their nest on your house is no fun. Instead of killing them with poison, consider knocking the nests down (and quickly running away) so they can disperse and build the nest somewhere else. Why? Wasp larvae act as parasites on many pests; hornworms are a good example. Wasps are a good way to keep other insect populations in check.

Succession planting. For certain crops with a relatively short time between planting a seed and reaping fruit (like bush squash, for example), once the plant gets established, I tuck in another seed near it. If the main plant gets overtaken by squash bugs and vine borers, I can tear it out after its first flush and have another ready-to-set fruit in weeks. In some places with a longer growing season, you can plant three or more rounds of bush squash. Their production is most prolific at the beginning of their lifespan, which is also a great method to increase yield.

Companion plant. The basic plants for deterring pests are marigolds, nasturtiums, and various herbs. I love to plant chives, garlic, herbs, and flowers bordering my veggie beds and fruit trees. In nature, there are never massive amounts of one kind of plant with no other plants around at all. An organized veggie garden is easier to manage but planting a couple of different varieties and herbs in the same bed with some garlic and onion on the edges and repellent flowers on the end caps can still be organized and manageable.

Rotate your crops. Many pests can overwinter in the soil. When creating a garden plan, try to come up with five or six different areas. They could be rows, garden boxes, whatever works for a particular garden. A rotation that allows for no crop (or members of the same crop family, like tomatoes and potatoes, which are both nightshades and affected by the same diseases) to be planted in the same bed in a five-year period is ideal, and for each bed itself to be rested once every five to seven years and left in cover crop. This may not be possible in certain gardens because maybe there is only a raised bed or two, do not let that be discouraging. Just do the best that can be done in any scenario.

Invite wild birds to the party. In some cases, birds can be garden pests. We will get to that later, but a healthy wild bird population can be invaluable in controlling insects. This applies to feeding them just enough so they stick around in winter, as they will eat bugs then too, which means fewer bugs will proliferate in spring. Put a birdbath near your garden (but not next to your toad habitat) and hang a bird feeder to draw them in. They are also attracted to bright colors and love to eat sunflowers. I suggest protecting sunflower heads with paper bags (remembering to remove them before any rain), as the seeds are beginning to plump if they are grown for food, but leave a couple uncovered for birds.

Use chickens, guinea hens, and ducks. All of these will eat lots of bugs and be incredibly beneficial to your homestead. I don't let any of them in the garden when the plants are young as they can get trampled easily and gobbled in a single bite. In the winter, the chickens spend lots of time free-ranging in the garden and will find and enjoy lots of the overwintering grubs. During the garden season, we keep them in a mobile chicken tractor that we move onto fresh grass daily. We let them out in the garden only under supervision. We have a small flock of guineas that are free range all year. We coop them at night to protect them from predators. Ducks are so darn cute; they do not dig, and their specialty is eating slugs. Keep a little kiddie pool for them near the garden and dump the water right on the garden every couple of days when refreshing the pool. Instant fertilizer for the garden! We had some ducks that wouldn't stop eating our peppers one year, so they are not completely safe.

BIRDS

Birds will eat berries and tree fruits and help control insects. They are beautiful and entertaining to watch and provide a lovely song for your ears and the benefit of the plants. Studies show playing certain types of music can help plants grow; birdsong must have a benefit. Birds love to eat fruit though, so let's talk about how to stop that.

Use netting. This is probably the best option. When your bushes set fruit, cover them with netting. Check the netting a couple of times per day, if possible; sometimes birds can become entangled and if they stay stuck for too long, they will die. This can also be implemented on fully dwarf fruit trees.

We eat sunflower seeds and we also leave some for the birds.

Startle them. You can use a scarecrow or tinsel, play loud music or an audiobook, hang chimes, aluminum cans, streamers from the trees, etc. Birds are smart, and these scare tactics won't last forever. Rotate them every week or so during the time when your fruit crop is close to harvest to be most effective.

Provide alternative food sources. When we start to notice the fruit is close to being ready or can see birds taking an interest in it, we put out bird feeders. Birds like corn, so planting a few corn plants near your fruit tree and timing it to be ready right before the fruit is a good bet. Also having food available in your landscape specifically for them is a good way to get them to leave the other food alone. For example, birds love to eat the fruit from a crabapple tree. Put the feeders away after the fruit has been harvested.

Utilize fruit bags. This is labor-intensive but works well for fully dwarf fruit trees. You simply put a little gauze bag on the fruit when it is small and wait for it to fully develop.

MOLES, RABBITS, GROUNDHOGS, SQUIRRELS

Get a cat that lives mostly outdoors. There are many other methods, even ones touted as organic (like putting chewing gum in gopher holes so they eat it and it becomes lodged in their digestive system and killing them), but helping the cycle of life play out in natural ways by introducing a predator seems somehow kinder than killing something just to kill it. At least with predation, that animal is helping to nourish another.

We also have to remember that the creatures that tunnel underground, although causing some major damage sometimes while doing it, help to aerate the soil and some of them eat grubs. Remember that every creature is part of the web of life and that completely getting rid of anything will lead to some other problem.

Be okay with little losses. Every year I lose a few plants to moles and groundhogs. It is usually early in the season. This loss does not make me want to eradicate moles or groundhogs. I try to replace the plants I lost if it is not too late; if it is, I count it as a loss and move on. If I started experiencing more loss from these creatures, I would get another cat. This year, cutworms were a problem in the early spring; they took out several tomato and cucumber plants and that was it. Always overplant. Plan on growing more than needed and make peace with the fact that there will be losses. If you have a favorable year regarding pests, plant diseases, and weather, there will be excess to give away, preserve, or sell. And remember that the benefits gained by being in the garden cannot be measured in bushels and pounds. Gardening is excellent for mental and physical well-being. This is especially true when you have a cooperative rather than adversarial relationship with nature. Nature also reminds us that we are never fully in control. Supermarkets give us the illusion of being in charge, but if the trucks and trains stopped running, the food would run out quickly. Knowing how to coax food from the soil is a valuable skill that, once mastered, will always be useful and be passed on to others.

There is *no* magical fix. This is so important to remember. In our culture we have been conditioned, by advertisers, to believe that one product should be able to solve all problems. That is the approach we have taken to agriculture and our health for generations and the cracks are beginning to show, aren't they? My children's generation is the first generation of humans whose life is expected to last fewer years than their parents. Companies are inventing many products, pills, and gadgets to try and figure their way out of the mess humanity has made for itself and turn a profit in the process. But the answer is simple: a holistic approach. A culture that observes their environment and bodies and then responds. More holistic results—and when I say holistic, I mean everything is connected and we need to honor that, not deny it. Fewer warning labels and long lists of side effects. I want to make my children proud, and I want the world they grow old in to be full of beauty and nourishment. So instead of a quick fix, learn something new. Gain understanding. Do not be intimidated by change; embrace it like a friend. There is much change needed now, so get comfortable with it. Share your knowledge and experiences. Let us be the generation that says no more poison on the soil, no more poison in our bodies. Wouldn't that be an amazing legacy?

Keeping seeds well organized saves time.

Saving seeds

Learning to save seeds is an important skill if you are serious about growing your own food. It can save money, and it also ensures that you retain a certain level of control over being able to obtain seed. Many people saving and using seeds of proven types in particular bioregions ensures the food supply is much more resilient than a few varieties of seed planted widely.

To begin, if you are planning to attempt to save your own seeds, you must start with open pollinated varieties. This ensures that the offspring (the next generation of seeds) will retain their distinct characteristics generation after generation if they are protected from cross-pollinating with other varieties of the same species.

There is a little learning curve for seed saving; there are entire books on just this topic. (I will include some recommendations in the resources section.)

ORGANIZING SEEDS

I organize my seeds in seed packs and envelopes in a binder with photo inserts. I like to add dividers, put seeds in categories, and alphabetize by category. An old CD, DVD, or trading card book would work well, and these can often be found at thrift stores. For larger amounts of seeds that I save, I place the seed in jars, label the top of the jar, and store it in a drawer or a box so that the seeds can be identified quickly from their labels. Having a well-organized seed collection makes planning a garden more pleasurable.

Propagating plants

When you learn to propagate plants, you can have a never-ending, free supply of your favorite varieties. There are different methods for propagating, and particular methods work better for certain plants. The main techniques are multiplying through cuttings, layering, division, or seeds. Some plants are as simple to propagate as putting a cutting in water until it sprouts roots and then putting the plant in the dirt. Learning to propagate can significantly reduce the cost of starting a garden and it makes it easy to gift or sell varieties of plants that have proven themselves successful in your area.

GROWING MUSHROOMS

Growing mushrooms on logs or inoculating mushrooms into the wood chips in your vegetable garden is not difficult, and the mushrooms can be harvested for years afterward. Spawn and plugs can be purchased online, or you can produce your own spawn, although that is a more advanced process. There are many varieties of edible mushrooms; however, there are also poisonous ones. Be sure to properly identify the mushrooms you consume; even if you have inoculated a log or other medium, you may still have an inedible mushroom appear. Do not ever consume a mushroom without being certain of its type.

Mushrooms are delicious, nutritious, and easy to grow. Once your log has been inoculated, you should get your first flush of mushrooms in twelve to eighteen months. The log will fruit several times a year (in spring and fall) and last for five to seven years. Shiitake mushrooms are delicious and have an almost meaty texture. Shiitakes can cost fifteen dollars a pound or more; investing in the simple equipment and spawn you will need to make them will pay for itself many times.

Shiitakes are so full of vitamins that they are used in traditional Chinese medicine because of their perceived benefits to boost longevity, circulation, and overall health. Studies have shown they help reduce inflammation when consumed regularly, and they also contain compounds that have shown promise in fighting certain types of cancer. They are a good source of fiber and protein and are packed with vitamins B6, B5, D, selenium, copper, zinc, niacin, manganese, and folate.

There are endless ways to prepare them, and they have a rich, savory, almost meaty flavor.

GARDENING FOR AN ABUNDANT FOOD SUPPLY

What types of mushrooms grow well on logs?

Many kinds of mushrooms will grow well on logs, such as various types of oyster, lion's mane, chicken of the woods, reishi, nameko, and shiitake. I am sharing specifically how to grow shiitake. There is not much variation in the technique when growing different types, but different mushrooms prefer different types of wood. Some species will also take longer to colonize the log and fruit. Shiitake is one of the faster mushrooms to grow as it colonizes the wood more aggressively than others.

Harvesting wood

Harvest wood in the fall and allow it to sit for a few weeks before inoculating the logs. For shiitakes, our favorite type of wood to use is white oak; we have easy access to it because it is prevalent in the woods on our property, and it has provided good results. The following types of wood will also work well to cultivate shiitake: alder, beech, ironwood, sugar maple, and sweet gum.

Make sure the trees you harvest are about four to five inches in diameter and alive (you will not get more mushrooms off a log with a greater diameter; they will just be heavy). After cutting, the logs should be stacked off the ground and rested for several weeks before inoculation. This allows for the tree's natural defense system to die back so that the spawn can colonize the log. In the south, where it is warmer, the logs can be inoculated throughout the season. In the north, logs harvested in fall that cannot be inoculated before winter can be stored and inoculated (or planted) in early spring. Dead trees should not be used as they will not have the food to feed the mycelium and they are most likely already colonized by other species of fungus.

Inoculating log with spawn

To make mushroom logs, you can use plugs, sawdust spawn, or thimble spawn. Plugs are considered easier and often recommended for beginners, but we prefer to use sawdust spawn as it colonizes the log more rapidly, which means the first fruiting will happen faster. It is also more economical to use sawdust spawn. Thimble spawn is sawdust spawn in plug form, which means fruiting will happen faster than standard plugs, but they are typically more expensive.

It is possible to colonize spawn, but that is a more advanced technique, so for these instructions, we are going to work under the assumption the spawn is going to be purchased.

LIST OF TOOLS AND EQUIPMENT

To make a shiitake mushroom log, you will need the following:

- Sawdust spawn or plugs. We like the variety from Field and Forest. We use the strain WR46 because it has proven itself successful in our region
- An inoculating tool, if you will be using spawn (not necessary for plugs as plugs will go right into the holes)
- A hammer if using plugs
- A drill with a corresponding drill bit. For this inoculation tool, we use a 7/16 inch drill bit (12mm); if you purchase a plug spawn, the included instructions should provide the corresponding drill bit size, 5/16 inch is common
- An angle grinder with a drill-bit adapter can also be used and will make the process faster
- Stop collar for drill bit or a piece of tape so that you can be sure to drill to appropriate depth
- Log
- Wax—we use beeswax, but paraffin wax can also be used
- Brush or dauber for wax
- Logs to inoculate

DRILLING AND FILLING HOLES

Drill holes about six inches apart in a diamond pattern. Use a ½-inch drill for placing sawdust spawn. If using plugs, the instructions should let you know what size bit to use. Make three rows of plugs on the log and space the rows an equal distance apart. An angle grinder with an adapter bit will make this process go much faster. It is okay to start with a regular drill. Use a collar on your drill bit or a piece of tape to mark how deep you want to make your holes. The spawn or plugs should come up to the top of the hole so they are easier to seal with wax.

Use an inoculator tool to deposit spawn, filling holes completely, or, put the plugs into the holes, pounding them in until they are flush with the surface of the log.

After putting in the plugs or depositing the spawn, use a paintbrush or dauber to seal each hole with a bit of wax.

HOW LONG WILL IT TAKE FOR A LOG TO PRODUCE MUSHROOMS?

After inoculation, stack the logs somewhere in the shade and off the ground. Use a pallet or rails to keep them off the ground and stack them like Jenga blocks but with spaces between so air can circulate. They should receive an inch or so of rain a week. If you get rain, this may be sufficient. Keep a coffee can or some kind of rain gauge near them and check it once a week or so to see if they need watering. If you forget to water, it's not the end of the world. It is most important when hot and dry. Watering deeply less often is better than watering for a few seconds more often. After about six months, move into the position where you plan to let them fruit. They can fruit as soon as six months; it will most likely take closer to a year and may take as long as eighteen months.

HARVESTING

When it's time to harvest, use a knife and cut close to the log. I recommend keeping the logs close to your residence so they can be checked frequently. Most mushroom logs fruit in the milder spring and fall weather and often after a rain. Our logs fruit two to four times per year. You can expect each log to fruit about a dozen times over five to seven years. Commercial growers have estimated that each log will provide two to four pounds of mushrooms throughout its lifetime, so a 5.5-pound bag of spawn (which inoculates twenty to twenty-five logs) can be turned into 50 to 100 pounds of mushrooms.

After harvest, store mushrooms in a paper bag in the fridge. Do not store them in plastic—they need to breathe, and the condensation will make them spoil. They can also be dried and stored for later use. Drying the gills in the sun will increase their vitamin D content. In fact, sunbathing them will measurably increase their vitamin D.

SHOCKING LOGS

If it has been over a year since your log has done its initial fruiting or more than eighteen months since inoculation and nothing has happened, you will want to "shock" your logs. This is done by soaking them in water for twelve to twenty-four hours. Often the log will start fruiting within a day or two when it is shocked, if not then, sometime within a week.

RETROFITTING URBAN AND SUBURBAN AREAS FOR FOOD PRODUCTION

These days, most of the population lives in suburban and urban areas. There is no reason why a few changes in these neighborhoods could not be implemented to allow food to be grown and available to residents.

Community garden in Chicago

GARDENING FOR AN ABUNDANT FOOD SUPPLY

An allotment in the UK

Rooftop garden in France.

Let's start with the suburbs. Many housing developments already pay HOA dues and have common areas, such as green belts, clubhouses, and swimming pools. Why is it so farfetched to think that, moving forward, subdivisions could be designed to include orchards and gardens, and perhaps even space for chickens or a few grazing animals? The residents could either be involved in the upkeep and maintenance or staff could be employed and paid to grow this food and this cost could be shared among residents. For existing developments, the subdivision could be retrofitted by adding edible perennial plantings in common spaces like green belts or along walking paths. HOA restrictions should also be relaxed to allow those who would like fruit trees, berry bushes, or a couple of garden beds in their front yard. Edible landscaping can be attractive. In fact, many plants people think of as solely ornamentals can also be used as food.

Some of my favorite plants to include in edible landscapes: Day lilies, artichoke, peppers, grapes and muscadine (for trellises), kale, chard, lettuce, okra, nasturtium, pansy, zinnia, viola, rhubarb, redbud, elderberry, chives, blueberries, rosemary, staghorn sumac, juneberry, fig, roses, lavender, runner bean, sage, moringa, sweet potato, pumpkin, and calendula. Some varieties of these plants will be more ornamental than others, so do a little research.

Large lawns are a tremendous sink of resources. They take time, money, and often chemicals to maintain, not to mention the tremendous amount of water they use. A suburb could easily be made to feel more like a village if people were bumping into each other in these common food-growing spaces or volunteering to work in them alongside each other. There could be community harvest days in the vegetable garden or orchard, or the work could be outsourced and paid for by residents who came to a common area to pick up their weekly provision boxes.

In urban areas the population density is high. There are typically spaces that the city maintains through tax dollars, but many of these spaces do not offer any sustenance and they are even sprayed with chemicals. There is no reason that fruit-bearing trees, vines, and bushes could not be integrated into public spaces along walking paths, in parking lots, in parks, and on the grounds of any institutions. When I bring up this point, I am often met with resistance because people tend to think of fruit trees as a mess, but they are only messy if they are not harvested. Community gardens are also an excellent solution in urban areas and more of them are popping up every day. I hope to see more perennials being included in these spaces, such as fruit and nut trees.

Institutions such as schools, prisons, hospitals, and nursing homes all feed people every day and use food services to bring in food, and much of the food is not of the best quality as far as nutrition. They also have employees that maintain the grounds, often with toxic chemicals and a significant amount of fuel used to power mowers and weed eaters. These places should all have their own gardens. In prisons, schools, and nursing homes, the gardens can be treated as clubs or extracurricular activities. Many people would enjoy being outdoors and working with plants. Garden therapy is a quickly growing field and proves that gardening, like equine therapy, can positively impact well-being. The food people eat is directly connected to their health, and children in schools deserve access to good nutrition. Incarcerated populations could benefit from it, and studies have been done on the impacts of nutrition and behavior and mental health. Special care should be paid to the food administered to patients in the hospital. Gardens, orchards, edible perennials that are also ornamental, laying hens, and, in some cases, even grazing animals such as sheep could all be easily incorporated.

Any public place that plants perennials should tag the varieties with a metal marker; this way the plants can be easily recognized and harvested by people, as well as propagated and more easily grown in the community.

If excess food is grown in these places, it can be donated to needy families through food banks. Every garden that exists in a community helps make the people there more resilient. We are importing too much of our food from other places, but that can change.

Rooftops can be the perfect place to grow food in large cities.

Decentralize and localize the food system

Currently, food production is extremely centralized. The best possible planet and human health scenario would be a return to decentralized, small-scale food production. Planting home vegetable gardens, including edibles in public works designs and community gardens, and growing food on small family farms are ways humanity can move toward a regenerative future.

Food can be grown on a terrace or patio.

CHAPTER 4

FORAGING

Mechanized agriculture enabled people to grow massive amounts of food. Later came engine travel and refrigeration; this allowed people to store foods for longer and eat foods that had traveled incredible distances daily. Today in many parts of the world, this has become the rule rather than the exception. As we reach the end of an era with a cheap and seemingly never-ending supply of energy, and as we assess the obvious damage this system has caused, we need to reconsider our dependence on far-away foods that require high levels of external inputs to be possible.

Eating foods naturally in abundance in the area where one lives makes sense on so many levels. Nature has a way of providing for us what is needed exactly when it is needed. Let's look at mushrooms as an example. Mushrooms are prevalent in shady and wooded areas, typically in early spring as we exit winter and fall and when heading into it. Mushrooms are an excellent source of vitamin D and one of the only non-animal and unfortified sources of this vitamin. Where else do people get vitamin D? The sun. The days are shorter in the winter, and we receive less vitamin D from the sun—a perfect time to eat more mushrooms. As you learn more about the medicinal aspects of certain foods and become aware of when and where they occur, instances like this become visible everywhere.

Foraging used to be much more common, even a couple of generations ago. During periods like the Depression, people grew gardens and used their knowledge of wild foods. Foraged foods, like dandelion greens, were important and nutritious additions to the diet. Foraging begins with the ability to identify plants. Then comes the ability to discern the edible from the nonedible. Those new to foraging will probably be surprised to find how many plants are edible, though some may require special preparations, have only some edible parts, or must be completely ripe before eating. Gathering food from the wild is exhilarating; it connects us with an ancient part of ourselves that has been sacrificed to the modern-day, plastic-wrapped, sanitized food on brightly lit shelves.

I foraged all of these in my front yard within fifty feet of the front door!

When beginning the journey into foraging, one must practice caution. I recommend obtaining field guides for the specific area you wish to receive foraging knowledge of, one or two focusing on edible plants and one or two general plant identification guides for your region. Why regular plants and not just the edible ones? Because sometimes a certain plant can closely mimic another, and to know what you can eat for sure, you should also know what you can't eat. In addition, many plants may not be widely recognized as edible, but with more research, you may find it is, has medicinal properties, or can be used in other ways, like as a dye, for example. I use my field guides and cross-reference them with pictures from the internet to be able to identify with 100 percent certainty. If I am not absolutely sure, I do not consume it. This can be intimidating at first; it may seem like many plants look the same. But with more practice, I promise your eye will become trained and you will no sooner mix up an edible and a poisonous berry as you would confuse an apple and a plum.

Along with field guides, take a notebook and a camera. Make notes about where you discover certain plants and keep track of the dates so you will be able to return. I like to go on forage walks of the same areas every month or so because as the weather and seasons change, so will the vegetation and the edible foods available. In a one-acre area of my property, I have found morel mushrooms (May), staghorn sumac (July), hickory nuts (September), wild plums (August), mulberries (June), blackberries (late June/early July), and passionfruit (August). Once you begin to recognize these edible plants in your environment, you begin to see them everywhere. And you realize that many people do not see them at all.

A few years ago we were at a small park in my town. My daughters immediately noticed a mulberry tree loaded with fruit. Under the tree were several weeks' worth of berries that had fallen. When people saw my daughters under the tree picking off the fruit and eating it, they drew a crowd. People gathered and children were curious, asking my daughters, "What are you doing? Why are you eating those? Do they taste good?" Some parents quickly rushed their kids out of there, seemingly freaked out by the weirdos in the park eating tree fruit. They probably loaded into their minivan and pulled out some berries they had purchased from the store in plastic because that has become more normal than eating fruit off a tree in the park. Other parents said, "Wow, you can eat those?" or "Oh, I have heard of mulberries but never knew what they looked like."

One mother even told me she had lived in the area her entire life and had grown up coming to this park and had never eaten a berry from the tree. She grabbed an empty coffee cup from her car and filled it to the brim with berries.

Wouldn't it make sense if most plants installed in local parks were edible? So much money, time, and fuel are spent maintaining these spaces, and there is the problem of a certain portion of the population who go hungry. What if there was available free food for the taking? The natural world can be incredibly generous, especially when given a little help. When we become familiar with the plants available to forage in our area, that can give us ideas of what to propagate more of in public spaces or our yards. These species are already thriving in our bioregion. If people included more edible species in private and public landscapes and learned preservation methods, there would be fewer reasons for anyone to go hungry. There are also ways to share across social media or through apps now so there would never be a reason for people to have fifty pounds of fruit that fell off their tree go to waste. Simply join or create a group on social media or post on an app like Crop Swap: come pick fruit and name the price. Or say it's free. Or create a trade: "Pick as much as you like if you pull the weeds in my garden or help me power wash my porch." What if neighbors also banded together and said, "You plant a couple of apple trees, I'll plant a plum tree, the Smiths can have a pecan," and then when it came time for harvesting, the neighbors could share in the harvest efforts and the bounty?

FORAGING ETHICS/ETIQUETTE

The most important rule to remember with foraging is not to overharvest. Never take more than you can use. If you are unsure of what a plant is and need to take a sample for ID purposes, take the minimum you can take and still be able to ID. Or take photos and make a note of its location. In the Western world, so much in the markets is available to us at any given time that it is extremely common to throw away food. It is estimated that about 30 percent of all the food that is grown goes to waste. Instead we can prepare smaller portions, save it for leftovers, freeze it, make stock out of it, give it away, compost it, or feed it to animals. When foraging, realize that this is a

resource you are sharing with other humans, animals, and insects in your area, so it is important to be respectful. Also, if you over-forage a plant, it may lose its ability to regenerate or regrow the next year.

Social media is a useful tool when learning to forage. I am a member of several local groups within my area, where we help each other identify plants and trade recipes. It is also an alert system; when you see people in your region sharing they have found certain edibles, you know it is time to look for them.

Always make sure the area you are foraging does not get chemically sprayed. Be aware that if you harvest food near roadways, it will have road pollution. Make sure to wash what you gather.

Consider going above and beyond not over-harvesting by guerilla edible gardening. Always choose species considered native and noninvasive to your area. Realize you may plant something that you will never be able to harvest; you may move away from the area, for example, but also be aware that as a forager, you are taking advantage of efforts that were not yours, whether from other people, animals, or natural systems like wind and rain. If you are harvesting things you did not plant, you should be okay with planting what you may never harvest. When foraging, be mindful of your environment. Realize you are entering the domain of many plants and animals. Tread lightly, listen, observe, and be respectful and gentle. Try to make as little of an impact as possible.

A FEW FORAGES

The following are varieties I was able to harvest in my own yard. Some of them may also grow in your area.

Chickweed: This plant loves cool weather and will often be one of the first things to pop up in spring, or one that stays plentiful all through winter in milder climates. This plant is high in vitamin

C and has been shown in certain laboratory studies to reduce body fat and prevent weight gain. It is also a useful plant to infuse into oil in salves and lotions as it soothes inflammation and itching.

Chives: If you have ever eaten store-bought chives, then wild chives should be easy to identify. They have a long, thin, tapered, hollow leaf. They will have a distinct oniony smell that distinguishes them from look-alikes. Wild chives have been used medicinally as far as back 5000 BC, possibly earlier. They are helpful as anti-parasitic, clear the sinuses, and heal burns and other skin irritations.

Clover: Clover is a common and recognizable plant. It is a good source of vitamin C and iron.

Dandelion: The entire plant—root, flower, and leaves—can be used. They are considered an excellent source of vitamins A, C, and K. They are also rich in calcium, iron, magnesium, and potassium. Remember that the plant will propagate via the flower head when it matures into a seed head, so be sparing about harvesting the flowers. Wait until plants are at least two years old to harvest the roots; otherwise, they will be small. Harvest the leaves to use in a salad, soup, tea, pesto, or even to add to homemade noodles.

Purple dead nettle: This plant is common and used all over the world for its medicinal benefits. It is considered anti-inflammatory, antibacterial, and anti-fungal. It is used to reduce allergy symptoms and lung infections. It is even used in poultices and compresses to stop bleeding. It has a mild flavor, and although it is a member of the mint family, it does not taste like mint. Toss it into salads, soups, or onto a flatbread or pizza. The little pink flowers have a tiny dash of sweetness and children love to forage and snack for them. Remember that the flowers hold an early spring forage for pollinators, leaving some on the plants.

Shiitake: This mushroom was harvested from one of the logs in my yard, although wild species do exist in some parts of the world. There are many species of edible wild mushrooms and many species that can be cultivated on logs, woodchips, or a variety of other substrates. They are a nutrient-rich and delicious food source.

Dandelion greens were used to add color and extra nutrients to these noodles.

It is easy to see why this fungus is called wood ear.

Wood ear mushrooms: Wood ear—also known as black or jelly ear—mushrooms are an interesting fungus. They do not look like a typical mushroom with a stem and cap but rather like an ear, hence their name. They maintain a crisp, chewy texture when cooked and they tend to take on the flavor of whatever they are cooked with. They are an excellent addition to soups and stir fry and they can also be boiled for ten minutes or so and then chopped and added to salads. My favorite way to eat them is with cooked ground beef or sausage, onions, and over easy eggs. These mushrooms also have medicinal qualities and have been used since 618 BC (the Tang dynasty). In China, they are used to treat breathing difficulties and sore throats, reduce fevers, and enhance circulation and overall well-being. They are also thought to be beneficial to people undergoing cancer treatment.

Violas, wild violets, Johnny jump-ups: Many flowers in this family are edible. They are high in vitamins A and C. They are also a beautiful addition to salads, cakes, cookies, and charcuterie boards. I love to add them to as many meals as possible when they are in bloom. They can be used pressed or fresh and have a mild flavor.

What is available to forage will vary widely by location; I hope within the plants I listed, at least a couple of them will be recognizable to you, as most of them are common. Become an expert on plants in your specific bioregion; who knows what delicious, abundant, and nutritious food sources you may be overlooking! You may have even thought of some of them as weeds. Consider that many species of plants considered weeds by those that would like to cultivate a perfectly uniform law are highly nutritious. Many people may be discarding weeds while purchasing multivitamins. What if your multivitamins could be harvested right in your backyard?

Whenever consuming a new foraged plant, start with small amounts to test for allergies or sensitivity.

Edible flowers make beautiful decorations for baked goods.

Consider going to your local extension office and approaching them about planting more edible plants, and asking that information be made available to residents about these edible plants either online or in print. If nothing is available, see if you can put something together. If you do not have time to do it for free, try crowdsourcing the funding from your local community or looking into grants. Imagine how world-changing it could be if information about local edible and medicinal plants was available in all areas: what the plants look like, where they can be found (generally and perhaps even some local maps with hotspots), and what time frame they are usually seen. Ways to use and prepare the foraged foods would also be useful, as well as best practices for propagation.

If we paid attention to what occurred naturally in our surrounding wild spaces, we could mimic and implement more of the thriving wild edibles in public spaces and home gardens, creating a source of low-maintenance free food within the community.

MAKE WILD VIOLET TEA

Wild violet tea is simple to make. Gather wild violets (remember to leave plenty for the pollinators), rinse, and put them into a jar. For every one cup of violets, use two cups of water. Place the jar in the sun, either outside or on a windowsill, and allow the violets to steep for a full day. Drink plain or sweeten to taste. My personal favorite is to add some mint. We add honey to this tea in the spring to soothe coughs. You can also combine the tea, sweetener, and some ginger bug (learn how to make a ginger bug in the preservation chapter) to make a delicious and beautiful homemade violet ginger soda. Serve the homemade tea or soda with a wedge of lemon or lime; when squeezed into the beverage, the acid will change the color from purplish-blue to pink!

CHAPTER 5

FOOD PRESERVATION

Preservation of food is somewhat of a lost art. When our diet is tied to what is produced in our region on a seasonal basis, there are periods of excess and periods of lean. Being familiar with different methods of preservation helps to maximize every yield. If you do not grow or forage your food, eating what is in season is still smart because it will be the least expensive. Buying large quantities and preserving them is a good way to stretch the food budget.

CANNING

Canning is one of the first things people think of when food preservation comes to mind. This method has many benefits: the food lasts a long time, it does not need to be refrigerated, and almost anything can be canned.

There are three methods of canning: water bath, steam, and pressure canning. Water bath and steam canning are reserved for foods considered high acid and have a pH above 4.6. This consists of mostly fruits and tomatoes. Some newer varieties of tomatoes don't have the necessary pH, so adding a little vinegar or lemon is recommended. Pickled vegetables can also be safely water bath canned because of the added vinegar. For water bath canning and steam canning, stick with fruits, jellies, tomatoes, and pickles.

For foods considered low acid—for example, vegetables, meat, seafood, or any recipes that mix high- and low-acid foods—a pressure canner must be used to prevent possible botulism. One benefit of pressure canning is that the food can be packed into jars uncooked as it will cook during processing. When canning a recipe with more than one ingredient, make sure to process the jars according to the ingredient that needs the most time. Also, the water level inside the canner should be a full inch above the tops of the jars.

Along with jars, jar lids and rings, and a canner, I recommend having the following equipment on hand to begin canning:

- **A jar lifter.** This will make it easier to remove hot jars from the canner after they are done processing.
- **A canning rack.** This is important for a couple of reasons. The bottom of the canner, because it is in direct contact with the heat source, may get too hot for the jars to withstand. Also, a rack (as opposed to a towel folded up in the bottom of the canner, which can be used in a pinch) allows the hot water to circulate better around the bottom of jars, ensuring the heat permeates the food evenly.
- **A tool to measure headspace and pop air bubbles.** Follow the amount of headspace recommended in the recipe. If there is not enough headspace in the jar, the food may ease out of the top. If there is too much, the food in the jar may discolor. In both instances, the proper seal might not be obtained. Using a tool to get rid of air bubbles is important because during processing, extra air will be pushed into the top of the jar, increasing headspace.
- **A ladle and funnel** for filling jars. This makes filling the jars convenient and leads to less waste.

Basic instructions for canning: Prepare the food for canning following a tried recipe from a trusted source. (See the resources section for some of my favorite books for canning recipes.) The jars, lids, and rings should all be sanitized. Fill the jars, ensuring proper headspace, and use a tool to remove air bubbles. Wipe the rims of the jars with a clean towel. Place lids and screw on jars fingertip tight. Carefully place on rack in canner. Water should be at least one inch above jars for pressure and water bath canning. For water bath canning, bring water to a boil and then your processing time begins. For steam and pressure canning, a dial or gauge on the canner will let you know when processing has begun. When jars have processed for the time in the recipe, release pressure, remove the lid, and carefully remove jars from the canner.

Do not place jars directly on a cold surface, as the quick temperature change can break the jar (I like to put the hot jars on a dishtowel next to the canner). Allow them to cool for twenty-four hours.

Write the date and contents on the jar lid. Don't skip this step! I always think I will remember, but I seldom do. Check to make sure the lid has sealed. If it has not, put it in the refrigerator and use it within two weeks. Sealed jars may be kept in a pantry and used within two years.

Applesauce

In the fall we go buy the "seconds" from a local orchard. The seconds, or non-fancy-grade apples, will not be in pristine condition but they make wonderful sauce. First, we wash all the apples by filling up the kitchen sink with water, adding half a cup of baking soda, and soaking the apples for 20 minutes. This will remove a lot of the pesticides. Then we rinse, peel, and chop the apples. The apple slices go into a large pot of water with lemon juice to prevent browning. Then the apples are drained and cooked. Add about a ½ cup of water for every 12 cups of apples. Simmer until apples are soft. Now is the time to add sweetener or spices. Sugar is fine and sometimes we add maple syrup, but most of the time the sauce is sweet enough. I use an immersion blender to blend the sauce until smooth; you can use a regular blender, a food processor, or leave the sauce chunky. Taste. Remember the sauce will have a more tart flavor when warm, so add sweetener accordingly. Using a funnel, pour the sauce into clean jars (4 pounds of apples will do about 1 quart of sauce). Remove air bubbles, leave at least 2 cm headspace, wipe rims with a clean towel, and put lids on the jars, turning the rings until fingertip tight. Using a jar lifter, place jars into a warm water bath canner. Process quarts for 20 and pints for 15. Remove jars from the canner and place on a towel on the counter upside down. After 24 hours, check the seal and put away. Put any jars that failed to seal in the fridge and eat within a week.

Simple quick pickled radishes

A quick pickle is when you pack veggies raw in a jar and cover them with an almost-boiling brine. Placing the lids on the jars while the brine is hot will create a vacuum as the jars cool, creating a seal. I don't trust quick pickles on my pantry shelf, but they can last for months in the fridge. This recipe is easy whenever you have more radishes, green beans, or cucumbers than you know what to do with. You could also look up the appropriate canning times for whatever vegetable you want to use and process accordingly to water bath or pressure can.

- 2 lbs. radishes, washed and sliced thin
- 1 cup apple cider vinegar (we use Braggs)
- ½ cup sugar (you may like yours with more or less sugar so feel free to add more or less to taste)
- ½ cup water
- 2 tsp pickling salt
- 2 tsp mustard seed
- ½ tsp ground black pepper
- ½ crushed red pepper
- 1 bay leaf per jar
- 2 pint jars (you can also do 1 qt or 4 ½ pints)

Pack radishes and bay leaves tightly into clean jars. Combine spices in a small bowl and add an equal amount to each jar. Combine vinegar, water, and sugar and bring to a boil. Pour brine over radishes, leaving about half an inch on top. If you do not have enough brine to fill, add more near-boiling water. When the jars are cool, put them into the refrigerator. If any did not seal, use within two weeks. For the others, wait at least a week before cracking the jars open; they get better the longer they sit. Eat within 4 months. When we finish the quick pickles, we like to pour this brine over a salad with a little olive oil.

FERMENTATION

Fermentation can seem a little mysterious and even risky; we have been taught that when things have been left out for a long time, or that when they change or develop an odor, they have gone "bad." In some cases, this is true, but the bubbling and distinct smell of fermentation are indicative of a metabolic process. Microbes in the food or beverage are processing the sugars and starches into alcohols, acids, and gases. This leads to a pre-digestion process, making fermented food easier to digest and absorb nutrients. In fact, fermentation increases levels of vitamins B and C and enhances biotin, thiamin, riboflavin, folic acid, and niacin. It also creates probiotics, which help digest and better absorb the nutrients in the food. Traditionally, people have eaten a fair number of fermented foods. Adding a portion to every meal can be beneficial to health.

It is important when making ferments to always use filtered, non-chlorinated water and clean equipment for best results.

Fermenting vegetables

Fermenting vegetables could not be easier. Simply combine vegetables, non-iodized salt, and filtered, non-chlorinated water. Put into a glass jar or ceramic crock. The vegetable matter must be kept under the brine level so that it does not become exposed to air, resulting in mold and rot. This can be accomplished with special airlock lids on your jars or weights for the crocks. I use rocks; I boil them and place them on top of the vegetables to stay submerged, and then check on my jars every day or so to relieve the pressure, so the contents of the jar do not overflow. Airlock lids are helpful because they keep the pressure inside the jar at the appropriate level. I prefer to do the manual check on the jars because I like to see how things are developing. If I use the special lids, I find myself neglecting my ferments and sometimes missing when something isn't going right. I keep them all together on the counter and loosen the lids and look them over in the morning when getting coffee or tea.

The amount of salt will be about 1–3 tablespoons per 1 quart of brine, depending on the type of vegetable, how small the pieces are, and your taste. Too much salt will result in the fermentation process not taking place, while too little will allow the bacteria responsible for spoilage to proliferate. When doing something shredded, like sauerkraut, I chop up small or shred, salt, and then put it in a large glass jar. I keep adding layers of cabbage and salt, using a tamper to smash the cabbage down in between, placing the layers to somewhat break down the cabbage. It will produce its own brine. When making a brine, I typically use 1.5 tablespoons of salt for 1 quart of water for hard vegetables (carrots, cauliflower, radishes, beets, onions, or garlic, for example) and 3 tablespoons for softer vegetables (cucumbers, bell peppers, zucchini). You can also add seasonings or herbs.

After putting your vegetables into a vessel, adding brine if necessary, and placing the weights and lids, make sure to keep them somewhere warm but not hot and out of direct sunlight. After three to five days, you will see bubbling in your jars. At this point, start to relieve the pressure if you are not using airlock lids. You can also keep them in a Pyrex or on a tray with a lip so if they overflow it is caught and doesn't make a mess all over the counter. Just how fermented you like your vegetables will depend on your taste. A little trick I learned: putting them in the coldest part of your fridge will halt the fermentation process, while keeping them in the door allows them to keep slowly fermenting. So think about that when placing the jars. Once refrigerated, I have kept ferments for as long as nine months.

Fermented pickles

The first fermented pickles I tried were purchased from a health food store (Bubbies was the brand), and I was hooked right away. I craved those pickles. They were a little pricey though, especially once my husband and children decided they all loved them too, so I learned how to make them at home. Read on for tips that will save you from the mistakes I made on my first jars and a recipe that will yield delicious and crunchy fermented pickles.

A wild grape leaf contains tannins, helping to keep the pickles crunchy.

KEEPING PICKLES CRUNCHY

No one likes soggy pickles. Here are a few tricks for keeping them crisp, whether fermented, quick-pickled, or canned with traditional methods.

Fresher is better. Make sure your cucumbers are as fresh as possible. Pick in the morning before it is hot and try to get them fermenting in jars that same day. If you do not grow cucumbers, then buy them at a farmers market early in the morning. Chances are they were picked that morning or the evening before.

Make them chill out. While preparing your ingredients and equipment, soak the cucumbers in cold water (throw in a few ice cubes) for at least thirty minutes.

Lose the blossom end. The blossom end of a cucumber has compounds that can make the pickles soft. It is the opposite end that was attached to the vine. If you are confused about which end is which, trim a tiny bit off each end—1/16 of an inch is enough.

Add tannins. Tannins are natural compounds that exist in certain plants. I have used wild grape leaves, oak leaves (do not use pin oak), and bay leaves—three to five per jar, depending on their size. I have read you can also use black tea, but I have never tried this.

OTHER FERMENTATION TIPS

Release the pressure. When fermenting, natural carbonation produces carbon dioxide. If not released, the pressure can force the liquid out from underneath the lid, making a mess. Keep your jars in a pan to catch any leaks. I have even heard of pressure building up to such high levels it can blow the lid off a jar, although this has never happened to me. I unscrew my lids a couple of times a day. If you are a person who spends a lot of time away from home, or you don't want to think about it, you can use special fermentation lids.

Everything needs to be submerged. It is important that all the cucumbers be completely submerged. If they are not, the part exposed to air will most likely spoil and this will risk spoilage of the entire jar. I like to take a large grape leaf and cover the top of the cukes, and then I use a weight to keep everything submerged. I use metal ice cubes because we just so happened to have had them on hand when I first started fermenting. Clean stones (boil them for fifteen minutes) will also work. There are even special weights made for this purpose.

Everything should be clean. Use clean jars and make sure your hands and all work surfaces have been wiped down.

The right temperature is important. Fermentation occurs easiest when the temperature is between 68 and 72 degrees. That is because that is the temperature in which the friendly bacteria that help create the fermentation thrive. I find that in the summer it is easy to ferment on the kitchen counter. Our house is drafty, so fermenting in the winter is trickier for me. Experiment with different locations in your home to find an ideal spot.

Try them before you try them. What I mean is, if you have never tasted fermented pickles, go pick up a jar so you know what they taste and smell like when they are done right. If you have never had a fermented pickle before, it may be difficult for you to gauge when they have achieved the correct amount of fermentation, and you may even be afraid there is something wrong with them when there is not. They smell and taste different than the pickles in shelf-stable jars at the store; make sure you know what you are going for and if you even like them. (Although, I don't know why you wouldn't like them; they are amazing.)

Refrigerate. Once you have achieved the desired amount of fermentation, store your tasty pickles in the fridge.

Wait for it. Once you put them in the fridge, wait at least a week (a few weeks if you can take it) before eating them. Trust me—they keep getting better.

Don't throw out the juice. That would be such a waste! It is high in salt, so although I do not recommend drinking it by the glass, it is full of electrolytes and probiotic goodness. It is the perfect thing to take a swig of on a hot summer day; even my kids love it. We have also made pickle sickles out of the juice. The jury is still out on whether probiotics can survive freezing, but they are still super refreshing.

Start small. I know, I know, you are ready to ferment *all the pickles*. Make sure you have this whole thing down though before you try doing huge batches. This recipe is for 2 quart-sized or 1 half-gallon-sized jar. Do a couple of small batches to get a feel for it. That way you can be sure you like your spice mixture and have a good temperature. Fermentation is easy, but there is a nuance that can only be learned by doing.

Recipe

- 3–4 pounds of whole pickling cucumbers
- 1 quart filtered water
- 12 cloves of garlic
- 3 tablespoons pickling salt (cannot contain iodine)
- 6–10 grape, oak, or bay leaves, depending on size
- 2 teaspoons mustard seed
- 1 teaspoon celery seed
- 1 teaspoon whole allspice berries
- 1 teaspoon black peppercorns
- 1 teaspoon dill weed or dill seed
- 1 pinch red pepper flakes
- 1 crushed bay leaf (omit if you are using bay leaves for tannins)

Equipment

- 2 quart-sized glass jars with lids or 1 half-gallon-sized jar
- Some kind of tray to put jars on to catch any leaks

- Weights for fermenting/canning
- Saucepan
- Fermentation lids (optional)

Directions

Soak cucumbers in cold water for at least 30 minutes. While cukes soak, make a brine by adding salt to water in a saucepan. Get it warm enough to dissolve all salt. Let it cool completely. (Do not pour hot water over cucumbers.) Combine all spices and divide amongst jars. Put whatever you are using for tannins in jars. If I am using oak or grape leaves, I like to get them damp and press them up against the side of the jar because it looks pretty. Sometimes they stay put as I pack the jar, sometimes they don't. Pack as many cukes as you can into each jar. Add weights. Put on lids, but not super tight. Within 24 hours you should see bubbles in your jars; this is good and a sign of fermentation. Do not forget to allow the pressure to escape a couple of times per day by opening the jars if you are not using the special lids.

They should be ready in three to five days or when they smell like pickles; that is why it is important for you to know what a fermented pickle smells like. They will be ready faster if the temperature is warmer and they will take longer if the temperature is cooler. Put them in the fridge and wait at least a week (longer if you can manage it) before eating them.

The spice mixture is a suggestion—it is what we like and can be played with and modified based on your tastes. Enjoy!

Kombucha and Jun

Kombucha and Jun are similar in that they are both produced with the aid of a SCOBY, an acronym for a solid colony of bacteria and yeast.

Kombucha is traditionally brewed with black tea and sugar, whereas Jun is brewed with green tea and honey.

Jun has a milder, less vinegary flavor and will ferment faster and at a lower temperature.

MAKING A SCOBY/BREWING TEA

You could get a SCOBY from a friend or buy one online; it is also possible to grow one yourself. To do this, you will need some kombucha or jun to act as a starter. Then create a brew with the same ratios you would use to make a regular batch, which is 7 cups water, 4 tea bags, ½ cup sugar or honey (depending on if its kombucha or jun), and 1 cup starter liquid (if brewing and you already have a SCOBY, you can reduce the amount of starter liquid to ½ cup). Combine almost-boiling water and tea bags in a clean glass vessel; I like to use a ½-gallon jar. Allow it to steep for 10 minutes. Add sweetener. Wait for mixture to cool completely, then add the starter liquid. Cover with a tightly woven cloth; a cloth napkin works well. I also secure the napkin with string or a rubber band. Keep it somewhere warm but protected from the sun. You can wrap the jar in a cloth if necessary. After a few days, the mixture will start to bubble slightly. Then a film will develop. After a couple of weeks, the film will lose its transparent quality. Once it has grown to about ¼ inch in thickness, it is ready to be used as a SCOBY. This will take about three to four weeks. It's that simple. Now repeat the process for brewing more tea. When you have extra SCOBYs, give them away, feed them to chickens or pigs if you have them, or experiment with them in recipes. I have seen people make jerky, sushi, candy, and fruit leather.

Second ferment

During the second ferment, the kombucha or jun is put into a sealed container (glass swing-top bottles work well for this) and they sit out for another two to four days to allow for a bubblier ferment. This is also a good time to add fruit or fruit juice to flavor your brew. There is no SCOBY necessary at this time. When your beverage is at its desired fizziness, move it to the refrigerator.

Making a Ginger Bug

A ginger bug can be used to brew ginger ale at home; it can also be used to brew many other delicious beverages. Making a bug is simple; it just takes time.

Start with 1 cup of water and 1 teaspoon of diced or grated ginger (grated may ferment slightly faster; diced will be easier to strain), and 1 teaspoon of sugar (I use organic cane sugar or turbinado). Cover the mixture with a cloth. Feed it the same amount of sugar and ginger every day until it becomes bubbly and develops a somewhat yeasty smell. This process usually takes four to seven days.

When the bug is ready, use ½ cup to 7 ½ cups of sweetened juice or liquid. To make ginger ale, grate more ginger, add sweetener to a ½-gallon jar, and add the ginger bug. In about three days, the mixture will be delicious homemade ginger ale. The same process also works with any fruit juice. Sweeteners like honey, maple syrup, and agave can also be used. I prefer to start the bug with sugar for the most consistent results, and then I often switch up sweeteners when combining bugs with sweetened beverages to make a soda.

Fermenting fruits to make homemade sodas

A homemade soda can be made out of any combination of fruit juices using whey, a ginger bug, or other starter culture. Use ¼ cup of whey in a half-gallon mixture. Use ¼ to ½ cup of sugar to taste and depending on how much natural sugar is in the fruits. Combine fruits and juices (blend fruit first to concentrate flavors), water, starter culture, sugar or other sweeteners, and salt to taste. Allow it to ferment for several days. During fermentation, the natural yeast in the mixture eats the sweetener, so the longer it ferments, the less sweet it will be. When it reaches the desired flavor, strain, and bottle. Keep in mind that naturally fermented beverages can become very carbonated when not kept cold. If you are not planning to drink your beverage right away, periodically open the bottles to release the pressure and take care when opening them to do so, pointing away from you in case they overflow.

FREEZING

Freezing is an easy way to preserve, and I use this method a lot. The downside of this is that if the power goes out for an extended time, the preserved food will not last long. That being said, I freeze a lot of fruits when they are in season. I also like to freeze tomatoes, greens, and beans. I prefer the texture and flavor of these items being frozen and thawed than canned.

When I freeze beans (green beans and other types of bush or pole beans picked young—I do not freeze shell beans), I typically blanch them first. This helps to preserve their flavor and texture. I do the same thing with greens. For greens, I use a muffin tin to freeze them into portions before packaging them for the freezer. For large fruits, I slice first; for berries, I freeze whole. I freeze them on cookie sheets first and then put them into containers. For tomatoes, I either dice and freeze or cook them down into a sauce or paste first and then freeze.

FREEZE DRYING

The freeze-drying process removes the moisture from food and freezes it, rendering it shelf-stable. While there is no data that proves how long home freeze-dried foods will last because freeze-drying equipment for home use is still relatively new, the companies that manufacture the equipment say it will last for up to twenty-five years. Another benefit of freeze-drying is that the food, when rehydrated, tastes closer to its original form than in a traditional dehydrator. The machines themselves are somewhat loud, expensive, and energy-intensive to run. However, having lightweight, shelf-stable food that can last for decades may be worth it to you.

DEHYDRATION

Dehydration is a wonderful method if you do not have enough space to store preserved food. By removing the moisture content from foods, you also remove a majority of the bulk. And there is no need to refrigerate. I like to use this method for herbs, tomatoes, meats (think jerky), and some fruits. It is a fairly straightforward process. An oven turned down to the lowest setting and cracked open can be used, but I have had the best results with an actual food dehydrator. It can sustain the right low constant temperature over a long period and has many racks to allow for a lot of processing at once. Make sure your food is completely dehydrated; it can then be stored in glass jars for up to five years and in some cases, even longer.

CURING

Curing is a method of food preservation that uses salt to draw out moisture. This process inhibits microbial growth that can cause spoilage. It is one of the oldest known food-preservation methods. Oftentimes specific herbs and sugar may also be included in the salt rub. Today the most common foods cured are meats. Egg yolks can also be cured. The yolks can then be grated and add an almost cheese-like quality to dishes.

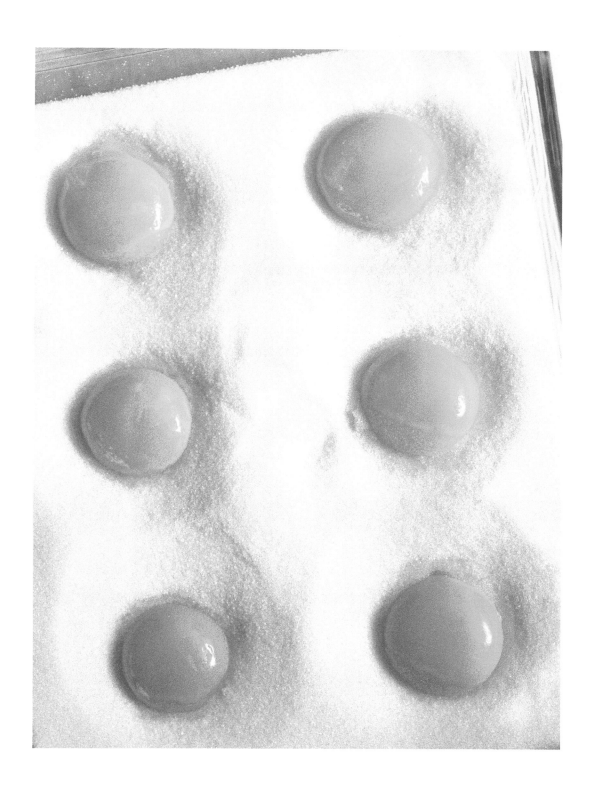

How to cure egg yolks

This is an excellent way to use up some eggs in the spring when we can't keep up with production or when we have a recipe that requires a lot of whites.

Spread about a ½-inch of pickling salt (non-iodized) in a glass baking dish. Use the bottom of an egg to put indentations in the salt—that is where the egg yolks will go. Separate the eggs carefully and place the yolks into the indentations. Gently cover them completely with salt. Cover the container. Place in refrigerator for one week. At the end of the week, remove them from the salt and rinse. Wrap them in cheesecloth or any clean and breathable fabric. Keep them separated by tying a piece of string between the egg yolks. Put them back into the refrigerator for one more week. They will be rich and tangy. They are delicious grated fine onto soups or salads, sliced and eaten on crackers, used as a topping for pizza or flatbread—the list is endless! They will keep for about a month in the refrigerator in an airtight container.

WATER GLASSING EGGS IN LIME

This method of egg preservation can keep eggs fresh for up to a year or longer. The eggs must be unwashed, fresh, and clean. Combine 1 ounce pickling lime per 1 quart of unchlorinated water. Distilled or spring water is best because the eggs must be unwashed to preserve the bloom; store-bought eggs will not work. Any egg purchased at a store in the United States has been washed. Unwashed eggs can be left unrefrigerated, while washed eggs cannot because removing the "bloom," a layer of protein covering the egg, allows bacteria to enter the eggshell. The chickens add the bloom to the egg in about the last ninety minutes before laying it, making sure that no bacteria enter the egg during the laying process.

When using the eggs, simply remove them from the solution and rinse. Then proceed as you would with any other egg unless you plan to cook them in the shell. In this case, use a small pin to prick them first to allow any built-up pressure to escape.

When we grow annuals, we like to focus on high-calorie, long-lasting staple crops like sweet potatoes, onions, winter squash, and potatoes.

ROOT CELLARING

The easiest method of preserving is to grow (or buy in bulk when these items are in season) foods that store well at a stable temperature for a long time. This includes onions, garlic, potatoes, sweet potatoes, other root vegetables, and winter squash. We have had vegetables gathered in fall last well into the following summer. If you have the space, simply storing whole vegetables is the easiest way to preserve. A proper root cellar is a luxury, but one can experiment with different storage methods. Perhaps a corner of a garage, a basement, or a mudroom might work. Many of these crops will store for a long time, even with high fluctuations in temperature, as long as they do not get frozen.

CHAPTER 6

BAKING AND COOKING WITH SOURDOUGH CULTURE

Learning to bake bread and prepare basic staple items like tortillas, noodles, and crackers is a skill you can learn no matter your budget or where you live. You need flour, an oven and stovetop, and a few other ingredients and basic pieces of equipment. Even though these food items are fairly inexpensive to buy, learning to make them yourself can still save you money. It also gives you more control over the ingredients and quality of the finished product. I always buy organic grains so I can avoid agricultural chemicals. This also helps avoid soy and corn byproducts, preservatives, and seed oils. Preparing your own food reduces the need for packaging, making it a more environmentally friendly option, and exposes us to fewer chemicals.

Using sourdough discard makes the grains more digestible. If you want the absolute highest nutrition content in your baked goods, get whole wheat berries and grind them yourself. Buying grains in bulk will also cut costs. I buy a mix of whole grains and pre-ground flour. I like to grind grains; I also like the convenience of buying grains ready to use.

As far as using the sourdough starter as a leaven, we have successfully used it in many of our tried-and-true recipes. Commercial yeast only began to be used widely in the 1900s. Before that, it was common for everyone to keep their own "starter." Anecdotally, some people with celiac or gluten intolerance have had success switching to sourdough bread or making sure their baked goods do not contain commercial yeast. Commercial yeast is genetically modified and lab-grown. Wild yeasts are all around us, and if you grow your starter culture, it will be full of natural yeasts in your environment. Commercial yeast comes from a strain determined to be a good rising agent and then mass-produced. Feel free to try out your favorite recipes that use a commercial yeast with sourdough culture instead. Commercial yeasts will rise faster, but a long leavening/fermentation process with a wild starter culture will make the result more digestible. For our bread recipe, we use 1 cup of starter to replace 1 tablespoon of yeast. Then we reduced some of the water and added more flour than the original recipe called for until the dough felt the same as it had in previous iterations. The loaf had a slightly different flavor and texture, but it was not diminished in any way. We make the following recipes all the time. They are all simple and I have the recipes printed out and taped to the inside of a kitchen cabinet for quick reference. I use them almost daily and so do my older daughters. I maintain my starter at 100 percent hydration, using equal parts flour and water. You can adjust the amount of flour in the recipes to get the right dough consistency.

MAKING A STARTER CULTURE

To bake with sourdough, you will need a starter culture. These can be purchased, but they are also easy to make yourself. To begin I recommend using rye flour. Once your starter is established, you can feed it different types of flour. I usually feed it with whatever type of flour I have on hand. I try to use organic grains. Also, white flour will produce less tang in the flavor of your culture than other types of flour. Start with 2 cups of rye flour and 2 cups of filtered water. (It is possible to make a starter culture with wheat flour, but rye will have better results.) Mix in a glass bowl or jar and cover with a cloth napkin, tea towel, or layered cheesecloth. You want it to be able to breathe, but you do not want any insects to get in or any debris to fall in it. Keep the starter somewhere warm but not hot. On top of the fridge is a good spot if your house stays cool.

Healthy starter culture will bubble and rise after being fed.

Feed the starter daily, at roughly the same time, for about seven days. When feeding, switch the starter into a clean container. Discard about half of the mixture and replace it with the same amount. Many recipes will give exact measurements or weights; I prefer to bake with sourdough by feel. The texture of the starter should be like yogurt, between regular and Greek yogurt consistency. As it gets more established, it will take on more bubbly/fluffy consistency. If it is too thick, I add more water. If it is too watery, I add more flour. With the discard, I make pancakes, waffles, biscuits, pie crust, etc. You may notice activity in your starter before the seven-day mark, which is good. I wouldn't bake with it yet, though. The good bacteria are colonizing and knocking back the other type of bacteria. If you reach day ten and have no activity, you may need to start over. Another tip is to place your sourdough starter near a bowl of fruit; fruit contains natural yeasts that can help colonize the starter.

Once your starter is bubbly and doubling or nearly doubling in size after you feed it (for several hours or overnight), you are ready to bake bread. Put a rubber band around your jar to mark where your starter is when you feed it to see how much it has grown.

Maintaining a starter culture

To keep your starter culture happy, remember to feed it one or two times per day (in the morning and before bed are easy to remember); it also has to stay warm, at least 68°F, to grow. If it is cold and you have difficulty keeping your starter warm enough, try keeping it on a heater on top of the fridge, near (but not too close) a fireplace, wrap it in a towel, set a hot water bottle beside it, keep it on a seed-warming mat, or cover a heating pad turned to lowest setting with a towel and set the starter on top.

Sourdough starter is a living thing, so go ahead and name it.

Your starter can be kept in the refrigerator and fed once or twice a week (although I have ne-glected it for weeks in the fridge and it has always been able to be revived). If you don't see yourself needing it for a long time, it is simple to dry your starter. Some people say this method of preserving is indefinite. Spread a thin layer of starter on a parchment or silicone-lined cookie sheet. Air dry over several days. Break into pieces and store in an airtight container. This is also a great way to set aside some backup starter or give starter culture as a gift. To rehydrate, put about a tablespoon of dried starter, 1 ½ tablespoons of flour, and 2 tablespoons of water into a jar, stir, cover with breathable fabric, and allow to rehydrate for about a day. Then begin to feed it regularly. It should be ready to bake within 3–5 days.

Following is my method for sourdough bread; although be aware—there are *many*. There is not one sourdough loaf recipe, or method, for that matter. Again, I do mine by feeling. Learning how the dough should feel and tweaking the ingredients to create that feel give me the most consistent results.

SOURDOUGH BREAD

I bake bread about once a week, and I keep my starter in the refrigerator when I'm not using it. I take it out the day before I want to bake it so I can feed it and "wake it up." I usually take it out in the morning, discard some of the starter, and use the discard to make something for breakfast or crackers to eat later that day. I feed the starter, cover it with a breathable cloth, and put it somewhere warm. Throughout the day, the starter will "eat" the flour and the water I add will bubble and rise. Before I go to bed, I make my dough for the next day. I put about 1 cup of starter,

2 tablespoons of salt, 3 cups of water, and approximately 6 cups of flour into a large mixing bowl and stir. I use a mix of white, wheat, buckwheat, and rye flour (more white and wheat than buckwheat and rye). Depending on the dough's hydration (this will vary based on the amount of each flour I used), I will add up to 1 cup more of flour, sometimes more, still stirring. This is a no-knead recipe. I add enough flour so the dough will not stick to the sides of the bowl. I cover for 30 minutes, then with wet hands (this seems strange, I know, but it works well), I stretch and fold the dough 10 times. I do this twice more in 30-minute increments. I then cover the dough with a damp cloth, followed by a dry cloth, and put it somewhere warm until morning. I feed the starter and put it back in the fridge to use the following week. You can also leave it out if you like to bake daily or a few times a week. This recipe makes 2 large or 4 small loaves; feel free to cut it in half if you want to make less bread.

The next morning, I shape the loaves and put them into banneton baskets. I add a good amount of rice flour into the bannetons before the loaves to keep the dough from sticking. I proof in the fridge for at least 1 hour but have proofed them as long as overnight (8 hours) in the fridge. After proofing, I dump the loaf onto a piece of parchment, score with a bread lame, and place the loaf (still on parchment) into a Dutch oven, cover, and bake at 500°F for 20 minutes. After 20 minutes, I take off the lid, reduce heat to 450°F, and cook for 12–15 minutes longer. Some people like their bread very dark, some like it a little lighter—this is a personal preference. Cool for at least 30 minutes before slicing. This may seem like a lot of steps, but sourdough is forgiving. Once I worked it into a daily rhythm, I started to prefer baking with sourdough to baking with commercial yeast.

To get a beautiful loaf of sourdough, some things are nonnegotiable. It must be baked in a Dutch oven to get the crusty artisan texture. Rice flour and a good bread lame (or razor blade) have to be used to make the scoring look professional.

CRACKERS

This simple cracker recipe is forgiving and extremely versatile. It can easily be made more interesting with various herbs and seasonings. My favorite add-ins are rosemary, garlic, basil, and thyme. When finishing, I brush on a little olive oil or avocado oil and sprinkle with salt and other spices or parmesan cheese. My favorite is garlic crackers topped with everything bagel seasoning.

- 2 cups flour—use whatever mix you wish. I like to use ½ white, ½ wheat. Sometimes I add a little rye.
- 1 ¾ cups unfed sourdough starter
- ½ cup fat (avocado oil, olive oil, softened butter, or lard—I love to use bacon grease, but each of these will yield a slightly different texture/result)
- 1 teaspoon sea salt
- ¼ cup fresh herbs or 1 tablespoon dried (optional)

Preheat oven to 350°F. Mix your dough. You want it to feel smooth, not sticky, so add a little flour if necessary. Put the bowl into a covered container in the refrigerator for at least 1 hour or up to 1 day. Divide this dough into 4 sections and roll it out thin on a piece of parchment sprinkled with a little flour. The thinner your dough, the crispier the crackers. A thicker cracker will have more of a pita-chip texture. Once it is all rolled out, cut it into squares (a pizza cutter works great here). I give my children some of the dough to work with, letting them make their own creations. I do this most of the time when I bake anything. They learn a lot and it is just as engaging for them as any other craft. I poke the dough with a fork to keep it from puffing. I then brush with olive or avocado oil and bake them until they are golden on the edges. I usually bake them for about 10 minutes, rotate the cookie sheet, and bake them for about 6 minutes more. It is all about figuring out your taste. The crackers on the ends where the dough may have gotten a little thinner will be ready before the ones in the middle unless you are precise when rolling them out. That's okay, just take the ones that look done off of the cookie sheet and put the ones that still need time back in the oven. Store them tightly covered at room temp for up to 3 days. They won't last that long. This yields 4 cookie sheets worth. Reduce recipe if you only need a small amount.

TORTILLAS

- 1 cup sourdough starter
- ½ cup fat, I like avocado oil or lard in this recipe
- 2/3 cup water
- 3 ¼ cup flour
- 1 teaspoon of salt
- Add up to ½ tablespoon dried or ½ cup fresh herbs or seasonings to add flavor, color, or texture (optional)

Combine ingredients. Dough should be stiff and like a shaggy ball. Either put it in the refrigerator for up to 2 days or use it right away. If using right away, cut it into 12–16 balls. Let them rest for 30 minutes. If you try to roll them out and notice the dough keeps shrinking, wait a few more minutes to roll out. Once they are the size and thickness you like, cook them in a skillet over medium heat. I put a cloth napkin in a basket or Dutch oven and as I add tortillas, I place another cloth napkin over them and I keep them covered, allowing the steam from the still-hot tortillas to gently steam the others. It makes a nice texture. Serve right away or store in an air-proof container for a couple of days. These will freeze well, but separating them with wax paper before freezing is necessary.

BISCUITS

- 4 cups flour
- 1 ½ tablespoons sugar
- 1 tablespoon baking powder
- 1 ½ teaspoons salt
- 1 teaspoon baking soda
- ½ cup frozen unsalted butter
- 2 cups active sourdough starter
- ½ cup buttermilk (you can use ½ cup milk plus ½ tablespoon vinegar if you do not have buttermilk)

Preheat the oven to 450°F. Combine the first five ingredients in a large bowl. Use the large holes of a cheese grater and grate the butter into the dry ingredients. Stir. Combine starter and buttermilk in a medium bowl and then pour into dry ingredients. Stir or work with hands until a soft dough forms. Turn out dough onto a lightly floured surface and knead a few times. Roll out to about 1 ½-inch thick (you can roll it out thinner and have your biscuits a little thinner too if you prefer). You will get about 12–14 biscuits. Bake for about 15 minutes or until golden brown. Check the bottoms at 10 or 12 minutes. It is easy to burn the bottoms of your biscuits. I like to do them on the second highest rack in the oven. These will keep in an airtight container for a couple of days, but they are the best hot out of the oven.

WAFFLES

- 4 cups flour
- 3 cups water
- 2 cup sourdough starter
- 1 cup avocado oil, liquid coconut oil, or melted butter
- 4 eggs
- 4 tablespoons sugar or rapadura
- 1 tablespoon + 1 teaspoon salt
- 2 teaspoons baking soda + 2 teaspoons water

Mix the first three ingredients and let that sit somewhere warm but not hot at least 4 hours or overnight. I mix it up right before bed. It should get nice and bubbly. Stir in oil, eggs, sugar, and salt until well combined. Right before its time to use the batter, mix the baking soda and water together and fold into the batter. I like to use a wooden spoon or rubber spatula for this. Pour the batter into a preheated waffle iron and cook until golden in color. This batter will also work for pancakes. This recipe is large because our family is large, so cut it in half for 4 people or less, or make the whole recipe and freeze some waffles or pancakes for an easy breakfast.

PANCAKES

- 4 cups just fed sourdough starter (This is a lot of discard. I usually plan this the day before, so I reserve what I need. Just fed will be less tangy.)
- ¼ cup sugar or rapadura
- 3 eggs
- 1 teaspoon salt
- 2 teaspoons baking soda
- 2 tablespoons warm water

Turn burner on to medium and add butter or oil to a pan so it can start to heat. Mix all ingredients. In a small bowl, mix the baking soda and the water and then fold them into the pancake batter right before you use it. Feel free to add more water or a touch of flour to thin/thicken your batter. In our family, some of us like our pancakes thick and fluffy, while some of us like them thin and almost crisp on the edges. This recipe makes a lot of pancakes. The recipe is easy to reduce, or you can save the batter for a couple of days in the fridge. You can also make the pancakes and keep those in the fridge or freeze them.

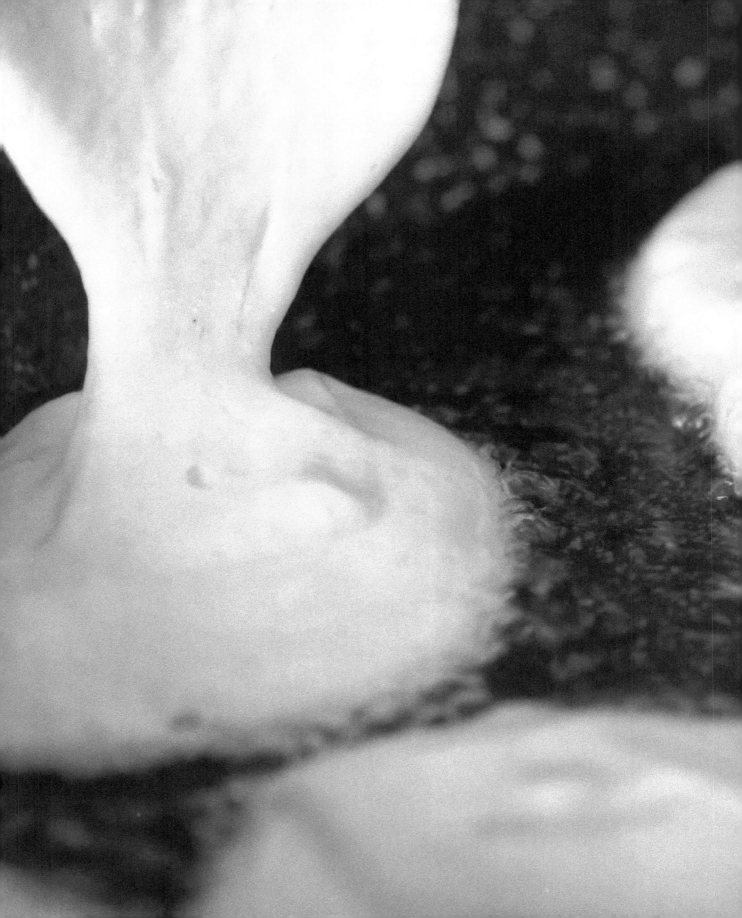

PASTA

These homemade noodles are one of my favorites to add to chicken noodle soup. They are also delicious with pretty much any sauce. The fun thing about making pasta yourself is you can choose to add other flavorings, colors, or certain plants for extra nutrients.

- 1 ½ cups sourdough starter
- 4 ½ cups of flour (I use a mix of white and wheat)
- 8 egg yolks

(This makes a lot of pasta. Feel free to cut in half. It also freezes nicely once dried.)

Mix all ingredients and work into a dough. It should not be sticky, so add a little flour if necessary to reach the right texture. Knead dough for a few minutes and then roll into a ball and keep in an airtight container in the refrigerator until ready to use. Let it sit for at least 30 minutes. I like to make the dough at night to use the following day. This allows more flour to undergo a fermentation process with the sourdough, making the noodles easier to digest.

Divide dough into 2 (or more) balls and roll out on a floured surface. Once the dough is the desired thickness, you can cut noodles by hand or use a pasta maker. Hang noodles to dry for at least 30 minutes before cooking (you can also dry them for 24 hours and store in the refrigerator for up to 3 days or store in the freezer). You can use a pasta rack for drying or hang noodles over the grills in the oven, over chairs, or you can create a loose ball or nest with the noodles and allow them to dry this way. When you want to eat them, put them into salted boiling water until they reach the desired texture. It usually takes only a few minutes to cook homemade pasta.

DUTCH BABY PANCAKE

Dutch baby pancakes are one of our favorite breakfasts. Regular pancakes are delicious, but when you have a large family, it can seem like it takes forever to make enough to satisfy everyone's hunger. Also, Dutch babies are higher in protein than regular pancakes, leaving everyone satiated. With Dutch babies, I can make 1 or 2, or double this recipe (double all ingredients except for butter) to make one in a 9x13-inch glass dish or large Dutch oven and it is enough. If using a glass dish (like a Pyrex), be sure the ingredients are room temperature so you do not put cold ingredients into a hot glass dish; this can lead to the dish shattering or exploding as glass does not appreciate extreme temperature changes.

- 6 tablespoons butter
- 6 eggs
- 2 cups just-fed sourdough starter (you can use unfed starter, it will just be *very* sour)
- 1/3 cup whole milk
- ½ teaspoon salt (reduce to ¼ if your butter is salted)
- 1 tablespoon of honey or sugar (I omit if making a savory recipe with the pancake)

Preheat oven to 425°F. Melt butter in a large skillet in the oven. It only needs a few minutes, so avoid keeping it in the oven too long so the butter does not burn. Beat eggs in a large bowl and add remaining ingredients. Take the hot skillet from the oven and wobble the pan so that the melted butter coats the bottom and sides. Be careful not to grab the hot handle of the skillet with your bare hands! Carefully put the Dutch baby batter in the pan and put it back into the oven. Bake for 14–18 minutes. Serve immediately.

We like to eat with berries, maple syrup, cottage cheese and jelly, cinnamon apples, lemon curd, powdered sugar, stewed fruit, raisins, and more; on the savory side, you can top with meats, cheese, veggies, herbs, or mushrooms.

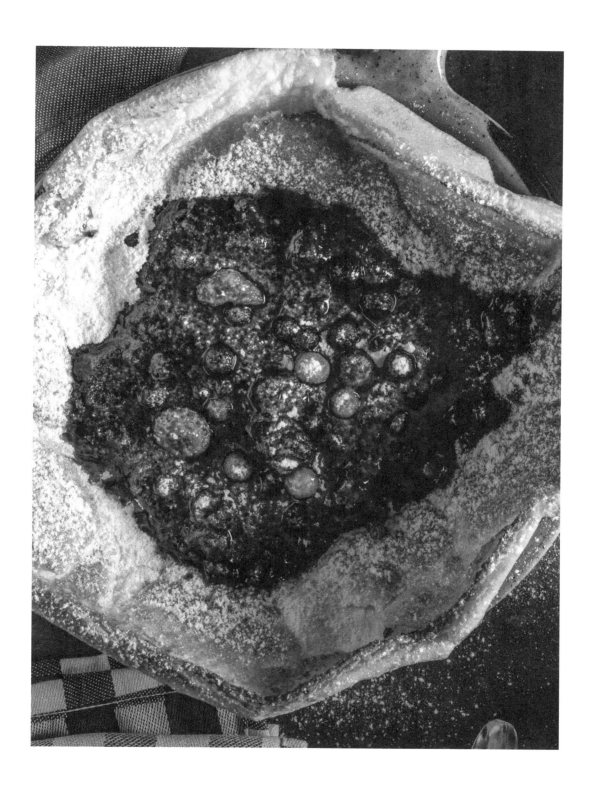

SHORTBREAD COOKIES

These cookies are so simple, with only 4 ingredients. Pressed flowers elevate them to something special that can be used to celebrate a special occasion or treat yourself and those you love to something beautiful.

- 1 ½ cups pastured butter, softened (straight from a farmer or Kerrygold are our favorites)
- 1 cup powdered sugar
- 3 cups flour
- ¼ cup sourdough starter

Combine butter, sugar, and sourdough starter. Stir in flour until completely mixed. Chill in the fridge for 8 hours or overnight. It can be made ahead and kept in the fridge for up to 2 days. Lightly flour your work surface and your rolling pin so the dough does not stick and roll it out to about ½-inch thickness. Use jar lid rings to cut out shapes. Press the flowers lightly into the dough; don't smash the cookie. I have found that flowers that have been pressed for about a day, rather than flowers that have been pressed for a long time or are fresh, work best on cookies. Bake at 325°F for about 12 minutes.

SAGE'S SPECIAL HONEY WHITE

My oldest daughter bakes bread every week for the farmers market. This is one of her bestsellers. Originally, we made this bread with commercial yeast, but now we make it with our sourdough culture. It gives the bread a slightly different flavor and texture, but our family and customers agree that it is delicious. It also makes the bread more digestible.

- 1 cup sourdough starter
- 4–5 cups flour
- 2 cups warm (not hot) water
- ½ cup olive or avocado oil
- ½ cup honey
- 1 teaspoon salt

Put water, about half the flour, salt, oil, and honey in a large bowl and combine. Add the sourdough starter (at this point, my starter will have been fed once to wake it up and is ready to be fed again) and then gradually add the rest of the flour. Pay attention to how the dough feels—you want it to be not sticky, but you don't want to add so much flour that your loaves become heavy. Knead the dough until it feels rubbery, put it inside a large, well-oiled bowl, and then cover. I use a clean damp kitchen towel or tea towel, followed by a cloth napkin. This helps keep the dough from losing moisture. Let the dough rise for 8–12 hours or overnight until it doubles in size. It will rise slower when it is colder and quicker when warmer. Make sure it does not get too cold; if it is not warm enough, your dough will have trouble rising. When the dough has risen, I turn it out onto a floured surface and knead a little, maybe adding a touch of flour if necessary. Divide it into two and put it into bread pans. Let it rise for 2 hours or until the dough comes up to the tops of the pans. Bake at 350°F for 28 minutes. Cool for 5 minutes and then turn the loaves out of the pans and finish cooling them on wire racks so the bottom of the bread does not get soggy. Cool for at least 30 minutes before cutting. If you want to try the commercial yeast version of the bread, simply omit the starter and add ½ cup water and 1 tablespoon yeast.

CONCLUSION

What does wealth mean to you? What images does the term "prosperity" bring to mind? Does it look like a mansion? Expensive clothes? Huge TVs? Fancy trips?

What if you work hard enough to be able to afford these things, but you put in such long hours that you never see your family and take such poor care of yourself that you develop a chronic illness? You take trips a few times a year, but the rest of the time, you work eight to twelve hours a day, eating mostly processed and fast food because you don't have time to prepare a home-cooked meal? What if the clothes you wear are made by children in sweatshops and the electronics you feel pressured to trade up on a yearly basis are manufactured at the cost of the environment and under horrific conditions? Can wealth be described as such when it comes at such a high cost to the environment, our health, and other people?

How many hours a day do you spend doing things that you truly enjoy? By truly enjoy, I mean things that spark real joy, not things that counteract boredom. When was the last time you felt or laughed deeply?

Reimagine with me a new definition of wealth and prosperity:

- I get to spend most of my time doing something that I like to do and am good at.
- The work I do to earn money causes no harm to other people or the environment.
- The products I purchase might cost a bit more, but that is because they are not subsidized, and their price covers their true and full cost. I know they are manufactured by ethical means; that is okay because I don't buy that many things. I understand the things I own require my time and energy to care for and organize, and I do not wish to spend that much of my existence devoted to "stuff."
- I use currency to purchase some things, yet I often trade my time, labor, skills, fruit from my orchard, meat I raised, etc., to others for goods or services.
- I spend lots of time with the people I love. I spend a lot of time in the natural world.

- I have the time to linger over long meals of nutrient-dense food that I know is chemical-free and nourishing to my friends, family, and me.
- I have the time to leisurely chat with a neighbor because neither of us is in a rush.
- I know with confidence I can buy available products at stores without worrying they violate my value system in some way because those products are not manufactured in my society.
- There is nothing on the supermarket shelves I would need to protect my family from.
- Food grows everywhere.
- Meat is raised with reverence for that animal; they are allowed to live as they would if humans were not involved except with more protection from predators and veterinary care when necessary. The entire animal is used and nothing is wasted.
- Western medicine is utilized in an emergency, but it isn't routine to go to the doctor all the time because people are healthy.
- We live healthily and productively into old age, elders are cared for by their families, and it is considered a privilege.
- Children are considered a joy and a blessing. They rarely complain about being bored because they spend most of their time in the natural world, and the natural world is recognized as full of wonder.
- Everyone has a garden, whether in their yard or in a community plot.
- People practice the golden rule.
- I take trips sometimes, but I know the place I live deeply. I know the names of all the plants I see and every bird that inhabits my area. I know the insects and the animals in the trees all by name. I learned all of this as a child. I know where to find berries in the summer, mushrooms in the spring, and the best spots for swimming and watching the sun rise and set.
- People have enough free time and brain space to educate themselves on any given issue, so they can support leaders and legislation that makes sense.
- When I head to the ballot box to vote for a president, it is a difficult decision because all the candidates are qualified and above reproach.
- Much of the country's economy happens locally because true craftsmanship and stewardship are respected and appreciated. No one wants things that have been

mass-produced and cheaply made and will break in one year. People buy things with the intention of keeping them forever and passing them on to their children.

- People are vibrantly healthy as a norm.
- Mental illness, obesity, and drug addiction are virtually nonexistent. When people suffer from affliction, they are treated holistically and personally.
- The households and communities we live in are closely knit and we do not let individuals fall through the cracks.
- Hard work is revered. Being too busy is seen as a problem to fix, not a virtue to achieve. The companies that have become large are still companies and not given the rights of an individual; they are transparent on every level, ethical, and can be trusted out of necessity since people wouldn't patronize them otherwise.
- There is no pollution because if a product requires pollution to produce, we as a society say no thanks. That is a product we can do without or can be made in a better way.
- A society full of people willing to pay more for far fewer goods produced using sustainable and ethical standards. They do not call these goods too expensive because they recognize them as valuable and are wary of "cheap" things. People buy things that are built to last and have no interest in disposable anything because they know there is no magical land of "away" where those discarded items go. To stretch budgets, people buy secondhand goods of higher quality instead of inexpensive brand-new items that will not last.

What do wealth and prosperity look like to you? Really think about it. If it means wealth and prosperity only to you, at the suffering and expense of others, is that okay? Why? What is the point? If luxury comes at the cost of someone else's quality of life, how is it any better than the slave ownership that occurred in the early days of America?

The truth is, it isn't. For some, it is complete ignorance; the corporations certainly do not go out of their way to shed light on the horrific labor practices in some countries. For others, it is callousness born out of a sense of entitlement. We may never have to set eyes on the people working day and night to bring us our luxurious lifestyle; that does not mean they are not real.

When we spend our money, we vote for the kind of world we want. You cannot buy things made from the spoils of essentially slave labor and say that you are for the ethical treatment of people. And guess what? The corporations running the world have become so greedy and morally bankrupt that it is virtually impossible to buy anything at a big box store that was produced in a way that respects people and the environment. A generation ago, pre-internet, people may have been able to live under this illusion. There is no illusion anymore because all of the information is out there if you want it.

This access to information has created a stir, a desire for a new paradigm. It is an exciting time with endless possibilities for restructuring old, unfair, unhealthy systems that were created under a reductionist mindset. Moving forward, a more holistic approach can and should be used.

What would society look like if it was designed for people's health, happiness, and well-being? What would it look like if we thought several generations ahead? Many of our systems, agriculture being one, have been designed around efficiency and maximized profits. While it is important for people to be compensated fairly for their work and enough food to be grown to feed the populace, it is also important that the food be healthy and not destroy the environment of the people it feeds.

It starts on the individual level because the power of change that can happen when many individuals shift their mindset and habits is enormous; it is everything. When many individuals come together and make big changes in their consumption habits, it is world-changing. As we work to make better choices for our bodies and homes, the trickle-down effect is that it is a better choice for the world. Everything is connected: humans, nature, animals, and a choice that negatively impacts one thing is not a good choice. We are all a part of one large organism. What is bad for your neighbor, even if that neighbor is on the other side of the world, is bad for you too. We, as a race of humans, can say no more. We have been fooled by clever advertising campaigns that tell us what we need, what we deserve, who we are. It's time to stop listening to them and giving them our money. It's time to regain personal self-sufficiency, thriving local economies, and strong, close-knit communities. The adage "the best things in life are free" is true, and on some level, we all know this. By choosing to relearn lost skills like food production, foraging, and food preservation, and supporting other people locally who are doing the same, we can bring economies back to a local level. Local economies lead to transparency and accountability, and encouraging ethical and sustainable practices. It also leads to resilience on a local and individual scale that doesn't exist when all of our most basic needs are dependent on globalized supply chains. Local economies are rich with the relationships that have been stripped from our current globalized economy that has become almost purely transactional.

Let it be our generation's gift to future generations to reimagine and recreate a better world. One in which all people, not some, can live a joyful and healthy existence on a planet that is respected and stewarded well. The fact that you have this book in your hands and that you made it to the end means that you are most likely tired of the status quo. I hope this book inspires you to live an intentional, authentic, and regenerative life.

ADDITIONAL RESOURCES

CHAPTER 1: PLANNING A REGENERATIVE FUTURE

Books

- *Family Friendly Farming* Joel Salatin
- *Restoration Agriculture* Mark Shepard
- *Tree Crops* J. Russell Smith
- *A Pattern Language* Christopher Alexander
- *One Straw Revolution* Masanobu Fukuoka
- *Small Farm Future* Chris Smaje
- *An Agricultural Testament* Sir Albert Howard

Films

- *The Biggest Little Farm*
- *Kiss the Ground*
- *Sacred Cow*

YouTube

- *Greg Judy Regenerative Rancher*

Instagram

- Cedar Springs Farm
- Ballerina Farm

CHAPTER 2: CHOOSING YOUR HOMESTEAD

Books

- *The Resilient Farm and Homestead* Ben Falk
- *Practical Permaculture* Jessi Bloom and Dave Bohnlein
- *Mini Farming: Self Sufficiency on ¼ Acre* Brett L. Markham
- *Micro Eco-Farming* Barbara Berst Adams

Instagram

- Hostile Valley Living

CHAPTER 3: GARDENING

Books

- *The Vegetable Gardeners Guide to Permaculture* Christoper Shein
- *Groundbreaking Food Gardens* Niki Jabbour
- *The Permaculture Market Garden* Zach Loeks
- *The Edible Ecosystem Solution* Zach Loeks
- *Gaia's Garden* Toby Hemenway
- *Garden Like a Ninja* Angela England
- *No Dig Gardening* Charles Dowding
- *Four Season Food Gardening* Misilla Dela Llana
- *The Frenchie Gardener* Patrick Vernuccio
- *Permaculture* Sepp Holzer

Films

- *Back to Eden*

YouTube
- *Roots and Refuge*
- *The Seasonal Homestead*
- *Stefan Sobkowiak*

Instagram
- Epic Gardening
- Learn to Grow

CHAPTER 4: FORAGING

Books
- *Healing Herbal Infusions* Colleen Codekas

Instagram
- Grow, Forage, Cook, Ferment
- Dr. Elderberry
- Black Forager
- Wild Food Love

CHAPTER 5: FOOD PRESERVATION

Books
- *USDA Guide to Home Canning*
- *The Farm Girls Guide to Preserving the Harvest* Ann Accetta-Scott
- *The Farmhouse Culture Guide to Fermenting* Kathryn Lukas
- *Wildcrafted Fermentation* Pascal Baudar

- *Wild Fermentation* Sandor Katz

Instagram
- Mark Joseph Philips
- Whole Fed Homestead

OTHER INTERESTING RESOURCES

Books
- *Beyond the War on Invasive Species* Tao Orion
- *Braiding Sweetgrass* Robin Wall Kimmerer
- The *Foxfire* series
- *The Botanical Skincare Recipe Book* by Herbal Academy Jocelyn Cross
- *Root to Bloom* Mat Pember and Jocelyn Cross
- *Sacred Cow* Diana Rodgers
- *Nutrition and Physical Degeneration* Weston Price
- *Nourishing Traditions* Sally Fallon Morell
- *The Harvest Table* Angela Ferraro-Fanning and Annette Thurmon
- *50 Do-It-Yourself Projects for Keeping Goats* Janet Garman
- *Keeping Sheep and Other Fiber Animals* Janet Garman
- *Winning the War on Weeds* John Moody
- *Teaming with Nutrients* Jeff Lowenfels
- *So You Want to Be a Modern Homesteader* by Kirsten Lie-Nielson
- *An Absolute Beginner's Guide to Keeping Backyard Chickens* Jenna Woginrich
- *Comeback Farms* Greg Judy
- *No Risk Ranching* Greg Judy
- *The Homesteaders Herbal Companion* Amy K. Fewell

Instagram

- Axe and Root Homestead
- Jill Winger
- White Hoof Acres

YouTube

- *Three Rivers Homestead*
- *The Seasonal Homestead*

Podcasts

- *HOMESTEADucation*
- *Doomer Optimism*
- *Simple Homesteading Life*

Websites

- Lowimpact.org
- GoodOnYou.eco
- EatWild.com
- Loconomy.org

ACKNOWLEDGMENTS

Books are a collaborative effort—not the words written necessarily, but the work as a whole. It doesn't come out of a vacuum; people in my life were personally helpful to me, and people I never met influenced me with the work of their lives; many of them I never interacted with personally, yet they were my teachers. So I will attempt here to thank them all. It feels inadequate because this work would most likely not exist or it would be different from what it is if it were not for the following people who helped me, shaped me, and taught me. I will thank them anyway.

The Southwest Institute of Healing Arts was the beginning of my journey into homesteading because their holistic nutrition program helped make me aware of the importance of the types and quality of the food I was eating to my health and well-being. This is what led me down the rabbit hole of farming and gardening. We were also lucky enough to live and work on a friend's farm for a short time; we learned so much through this experience. Thank you, Emily, for the many meals you prepared for our family, and thanks to Lindsey, only seven years old at the time, who gave me my first gardening lessons. She was a wise and patient teacher. Your family showed us a different way of life and we are forever grateful.

My gardening path might have been different if I had not read books like *Gaia's Garden* by Toby Hemenway, *Micro Eco-Farming* by Barbara Berst Adams, and *The Apple Grower* by Michael Philips. Books like *You Can Farm* and *Family Friendly Farming* by Joel Salatin helped us imagine a way of life that would include earning a portion of our income from the land and making sure we were honest with ourselves about how much work it would be. A few years later, *The Holistic Orchard* (also by Philips) and the *Resilient Farm and Homestead* by Ben Falk came along. These books resonated with me and "just made sense." They also taught me an immeasurable amount. I read them early on in my days of homesteading and food-growing and they were formative for me. Later, *The Permaculture Market Garden* (Zach Loeks) and *Practical Permaculture* (Jessi Bloom and Dave Boehnlein) helped to further expand my knowledge. The permaculture design course I took at Oregon State University taught me and challenged in ways that I would not have challenged myself, transforming me from a person who loved permaculture and had practiced it on my own into someone capable of designing for others. Much gratitude to my instructors, Andrew Millison and Kelda Lorax.

Thank you to Jane Kinney Denning, acquisitions editor, for seeing something in my work that she thought was of value and helping me to refine a vision for this book. Thanks to my editor Lisa McGuinness and all the other people at Mango Publishing who helped turn my words into a real, actual book.

Last but definitely not least, I want to thank some people in my personal life. My friend Amanda, who said to me after I expressed my desire to start a blog that would help people make better choices about what they ate and learn to be more self-sufficient, "Why don't you just do it?" My friend Hutton, who acted as an accountability coach in the early days of starting my blog, was always so full of encouragement. My sister Rebecca, who has steadfastly believed in me all of my life, what a powerful gift that is. My children, who understood "Mommy needing to get work done" and actively cheered me on. And my husband, who did the hands-on work of picking up the slack in our home and gave me, and continues to give me, the space I needed to do the work I love.

ABOUT THE AUTHOR

Roxanne Ahern studied holistic nutrition at Southwest Institute of Healing Arts and permaculture design at Oregon State University. She has been growing food and raising livestock for more than twelve years. She is passionate about health and sustainability and acts as a consultant for nutrition and homesteading and designs edible landscapes. Roxanne lives on her homestead in the Southeast with her husband and five daughters, where they wildcraft, grow food, and raise chickens, sheep, goats, pigs, ducks, and Guinea fowl.

HOLISTIC HOMESTEADING

P . S .

I genuinely hope you enjoyed this book! I am so grateful you chose to read it. I love hearing from readers, so feel free to follow along with our homestead journey on Instagram (@happyholistichomestead), Facebook (Happy Holistic Homestead), Twitter (@happyholistichs), or on our blog/website at Happyholistichomestead.com. If you loved this book, it would mean a lot to me if you took a few minutes to review it on Amazon (or anywhere else on the web you can find it). Positive reviews can make a difference in the number of copies a book sells, so if you want more people to read this book, a positive review can help make that happen. I wish you the best of luck on your journey to carving out a more holistic life.

yellow pear press

Yellow Pear Press, established in 2015, publishes inspiring, charming, clever, distinctive, playful, imaginative, beautifully-designed lifestyle books, cookbooks, literary fiction, notecards, and journals with a certain *joie de vivre* in both content and style. Yellow Pear Press books have been honored by the Independent Publisher Book (IPPY) Awards, National Indie Excellence Awards, Independent Press Awards, and International Book Awards. Reviews of our titles have appeared in Kirkus Reviews, Foreword Reviews, Booklist, Midwest Book Review, San Francisco Chronicle, and New York Journal of Books, among others. Yellow Pear Press joined forces with Mango Publishing in 2020, both with the vision to continue publishing clever and innovative books. The fact that they're both named after fruit is a total coincidence.

We love hearing from our readers, so please stay in touch with us and follow us at:
Facebook: Yellow Pear Press
Twitter: @yellowpearpress
Instagram: @yellowpearpress
Pinterest: yellowpearpress
Website: www.yellowpearpress.com

CPSIA information can be obtained
at www.ICGtesting.com
Printed in the USA
JSHW061150210622
27317JS00005B/17